Social Protection Floors

Social Protection Floors

Volume 2:
Innovations to extend coverage

Edited by Isabel Ortiz, Valérie Schmitt, Loveleen De

International Labour Organization

Social Protection Floors. Volume 2: Innovations to extend coverage
Isabel Ortiz, Valérie Schmitt, Loveleen De (Eds.)

© International Labour Organization 2016, Social Protection Department.
ISBN: 978-1-365-58584-5

We should work together under a common policy approach – the social protection floor – to promote a very clear outcome. No one should live below a certain income level.

Ban Ki-moon,
United Nations Secretary General

Social protection floors for a fair and inclusive globalization.

Michelle Bachelet,
former Executive Director of UNWOMEN and
President of Chile

Acknowledgements

This book is the second volume of the series on "Social Protection Floors" published by the ILO. The editors would like to express their sincere thanks and gratitude to all the people who have contributed to this volume through their authorship, research and analysis. The different chapters of this volume are authored by and benefit from contributions by various people (in alphabetical order):

Aidi Hu, Senior Social Protection Specialist for East Asia, ILO; Cheng Boon Ong, former Consultant for the ILO; Clara van Panhuys, Social Protection Officer, ILO; Daria Copil, formerly of the ILO; James Canonge, Social Protection Officer, ILO; Fabio Durán-Valverde, Senior Social Protection Specialist, ILO; José Francisco Ortiz-Vindas, ILO; Kenichi Hirose, Senior Social Protection Specialist for Central and Eastern Europe, ILO; Lara Polus, formerly of the ILO; Stefan Urban, Actuary, ILO; Thea Westphal, Consultant for the ILO and Thibault van Langenhove, Social Protection Policy Officer, ILO.

The editors also value the support received from various people in reviewing the chapters (in alphabetical order):

Anne Drouin, Chief of the Public Finance, Actuarial and Statistics Branch, ILO; Celine Peyron-Bista, Chief Technical Advisor, ILO; Christina Behrendt, Senior Social Protection Specialist, ILO; Clara van Panhuys, Social Protection Officer, ILO; Karuna Pal, Senior Coordinator Budget and Resource Management, ILO; Helmut Schwarzer, Senior Social Protection Specialist, ILO Mexico; Hiroshi Yamabana, Senior Actuary, ILO; James Canonge, Social Protection Officer, ILO and Martin Hirsch, Director General of the Assistance publique – Hôpitaux de Paris and former High Commissioner for Active Solidarity Against Poverty.

Last but not the least, the editors express their gratitude to the Agence Française de Développement (AFD) for their collaboration with the ILO on the chapters related to climate change and to Jessica Vechbanyongratana, Assistant Professor at Chulalongkorn University, Thailand and Victoria Giroud-Castiella, Social Protection Officer, ILO for their support to the series on "Social Protection Floors".

The editors of this volume are Isabel Ortiz, Director of the Social Protection Department, ILO; Valérie Schmitt, Chief of Social Policy, Governance and Standards, ILO and Loveleen De, Social Protection Policy Officer, ILO.

Contents

List of figures

List of tables

Introduction

Social protection floors: A global consensus

Social protection allows for a life in dignity. However, it is still a privilege for far too few. Many older persons do not receive pensions and few children, mothers and persons with disabilities get the support that they need. Too many people are poor and without jobs, left behind by prosperous societies. This massive social protection gap is not acceptable from a human rights perspective. It is also a missed opportunity from a developmental point of view.

Access to social protection is not only a moral imperative, enshrined in the Universal Declaration of Human Rights and other international agreements, but also a critical ingredient for economic growth. Investing for an educated and healthy workforce can foster transitions from low productivity jobs to decent, high productivity jobs. Social protection serves as a stabilizer in times of crisis, providing much-needed income that can maintain or even boost demand and consumption during economic downturns. These positive impacts on workers and the resilience of national economies make social protection systems an attractive investment for many countries and one that will support them in their efforts towards sustainable economic growth.

In a time of rising inequalities, social protection is an indispensable tool for creating inclusive and equitable societies, in which redistribution and solidarity play important roles to build and maintain a lasting social peace.

It is for these reasons that social protection systems and floors are a key priority for the ILO and UN member States. In 2012, the Social Protection Floors Recommendation (No. 202) was adopted unanimously member States (see Annex 1). This Recommendation is the only internationally agreed treaty that reflects a global consensus on universal social protection. It defines social protection floors (SPFs) as a set of social security guarantees that ensure, at a minimum, that all people have access to social protection at adequate benefit levels – or income security. Social protection floors typically include, but are not limited to, cash transfers for children, maternity benefits, disability pensions, support for those without jobs, old-age pensions as well as access to essential health care.

The roll-out of social protection floors is one of the key priorities of the United Nations' 17 Sustainable Development Goals (SDGs), adopted by all countries across the world in 2015. The 2030 development agenda (see Annex 2) calls for efforts to eradicate poverty and equalize income distribution so that as countries continue to develop, the benefits of growth can be enjoyed by all. Specifically, SDG 1.3 commits States to implement nationally appropriate social protection systems and measures for all, including floors, by 2030.[1] By establishing universal social protection systems, including social protection floors, countries can ensure that no one is left behind and that prosperity is shared.

Since the end of the 19th century, significant progress has been made in building social security or social protection systems.[2] From early steps taken in a number of pioneering European countries, the scope of social security, measured by the number of areas covered by social protection systems,[3] was extended at

---

[1] Countries will track progress till 2030 on the proportion of population covered by social protection systems and floors, including coverage of women and men, children, unemployed persons, older persons, persons with disabilities, pregnant women, newborns, victims of work injuries, the poor and the vulnerable.
[2] In this series, social protection and social security are used interchangeably.
[3] Countries tend to build their national social security systems in sequential steps, depending on circumstances and priorities. In many cases, countries have first addressed the area of employment injury; followed by the introduction of old-age pensions, disability and

an impressive pace, including the creation of ministries of labour, ministries of social security and welfare and other relevant institutions. Today, the majority of countries have social protection schemes established by law as well as a myriad of cash transfers, albeit in many developing countries, the schemes benefit only a minority of the population.

Against this backdrop, countries across the world have prioritized the expansion of coverage. From a historical perspective, it is the right time. Today, India is richer than Germany was when it introduced social insurance for all workers in the 1880s and Indonesia is richer than the United States was when it enacted the Social Security Act in 1935. Many developing countries have successfully established universal social protection schemes, providing evidence to the rest of the world that expanding coverage to all is not only necessary but also feasible.

This is because social protection works. It is not a form of charity or a way of giving a few dole-outs to the most vulnerable. Social protection involves strategically designing and implementing comprehensive national systems. Such systems can raise productivity by investing in the workforce; ensure national consumption through higher incomes; and reduce poverty, inequality and political instability. In just a few years, China has put in place nearly universal pensions. Developing countries such as Argentina, Bolivia, Botswana, Brazil, Cabo Verde, Kazakhstan, Lesotho, Maldives, Mongolia, Namibia, Nepal, South Africa, Thailand, Timor Leste and Uruguay, among others, have established universal social protection schemes. Many governments are expanding the coverage of pensions for older

---

survivor benefits; and the later introduction of sickness, health-care and maternity coverage. Benefits for children and families and unemployment benefits are often implemented last (see the World Social Protection Report 2014-15. Geneva, ILO).

persons, disability and maternity benefits, support for people without jobs and cash transfers for children.

Most interestingly, developing countries are expanding coverage in very innovative ways. We try to reflect the richness of the new 21stcentury approaches in the volumes in this series.

About this volume: Innovations to extend coverage

This is the second volume of a series on successful experiences in building social protection floors. This volume showcases 13 experiences from 11 countries and one region which have developed innovative solutions to extend social protection coverage.

People excluded from social protection usually include self-employed workers, informal economy and rural workers and their families, domestic workers, migrant workers, people at risk from natural disasters and many others. These groups, often cited as "difficult to cover" groups face numerous challenges in availing social protection benefits from traditionally designed systems. They may have irregular income patterns that make the payment of monthly contributions difficult. They may live in remote areas and therefore, may not be able to travel to the nearest social protection institution to collect their entitlements. They may not possess the basic documents, such as an identity card or birth certificate, which are required to register for social protection schemes. They may not be in a position to fight for their social protection rights due to lack of information or representation. Extending social protection to these groups of people requires not just political will but also innovative approaches.

Many developing and middle-income countries have designed and implemented innovative yet practical solutions to extend coverage to these groups. In less than ten years, through complementary policy measures, China expanded coverage to almost all its 270 million rural migrant workers previously excluded from social protection schemes. Since 2009, El Salvador has made massive investments to cover vulnerable people across their life cycle, through a coherent set of non-contributory programmes. Uruguay's Monotax system enabled the extension of social protection coverage to self-employed workers and workers in small enterprises, by simplifying and unifying the collection of taxes and social contributions.

In some countries, external events such as industrial accidents and natural disasters have helped to mobilize national consensus on the necessity of expanding social protection. In Bangladesh, a compensation scheme was implemented for victims of the Rana Plaza accident, with support from the ILO. It raised awareness on the importance of employment injury insurance (EII) to better protect workers and their dependents as well as enterprises from the financial consequences of major industrial accidents. The occurrence of natural calamities such as typhoons in the Philippines and repeated droughts and floods in the Sahel region have led to specific strategies and programmes directed at building the resilience of their populations through social protection. To offset the effects of climate change on people, there is a need for a "just transition" through the development of social protection measures. As part of anti-deforestation measures by the government, Brazil and China provide cash payments to people in relation to forest conservation and ecological performance.

Countries have also adopted Innovative designs for the right mix of income security and activation measures for the working poor, seasonal workers and long-term unemployed persons. Romania provides a cold weather allowance to construction workers during the interruption of their work in winter, thereby creating an incentive for workers and their skills to remain in the domestic labour market. France's Active Solidarity Income was created in 2008 with the objectives of addressing poverty among the working poor and providing income security to unemployed persons while reducing the financial disincentives to return to work. India's Mahatma Gandhi National Rural Employment

6. Innovations to extend coverage

Guarantee Scheme, introduced in 2005, guarantees work for rural households while creating assets and strengthening local governance. South Africa provides a Child Support Grant to poor families with children which, interestingly, had long-term health and education related impacts on children and enabled mothers to participate in the labour market. Malaysia's Return to Work programme helps injured workers and workers with disabilities to recover and re-join the workforce as early as possible.

The approaches of different countries presented in this volume demonstrate that innovations are critical for countries who aim to extend social protection to uncovered groups of people. These experiences can serve as a source of inspiration to all countries that have prioritized the development of nationally appropriate social protection systems and measures for all, including floors, as part of their SDG implementation plans. The diversity of examples shows that there is no "one size fits all" approach to the development of universal social protection. Indeed, each country needs to find its own path in line with its vision of society. The number of country cases indicates that there is great scope for South-South exchange in the extension of social protection.

It is our hope that this volume will give readers concrete ideas on extending social protection to all and, in a few years, many more countries will be able to share their experiences with social protection policy makers from the Global South.

1

Bangladesh: Employment injury insurance[4]

Tragic industrial accidents in Bangladesh over the past years, such as the Rana Plaza collapse, with 1,134 deaths and around 2,500 injured, brought international attention and highlighted the need to improve health and safety standards and to put a reliable system in place that compensates and supports victims and their dependents in cases of work accident.

Since the Rana Plaza accident on 24 April 2013, the Government of Bangladesh, employers, trade unions and non-governmental organizations (NGOs) formed the Rana Plaza Coordination Committee (RPCC) that, with the ILO acting as a neutral chair and the ILO's technical assistance, developed a compensation scheme for the victims, their families and dependants.

1. Main lessons learned

- The tragic events in Bangladesh shed light on the shortcomings of the existing compensation system in cases of workplace accidents and put enormous pressure on national and international stakeholders to develop a compensation scheme for the victims, their families and dependants.
- These events also raised awareness on the need to establish an employment injury insurance (EII) scheme in Bangladesh to better protect workers and their

---

[4] This chapter was authored by Stefan Urban of the ILO and reviewed by Hiroshi Yamabana, Anne Drouin and Valérie Schmitt of the ILO. It was first published in September 2016.

dependents by providing periodical benefits in cash and in kind in cases of work-related accidents and occupational disease.

- Both employers and the broader buyers' community progressively understood that contrary to employers' liability programmes, an EII scheme, through collective risk pooling, not only protects workers and their dependents, but also employers against the financial consequences of catastrophic accidents. EII also reduces the risks for brands and buyers that are no longer held responsible for compensating injured workers in factories.

2. How was the Rana Plaza Compensation scheme developed?

The Rana Plaza catastrophe in Bangladesh in April 2013 was a wake-up call for the industry. This accident, which took the lives of more than 1,134 workers and injured around 2,500 others, made people realize that many workers still today lack adequate protection in the case of work injury.

In an initial effort after the collapse of the Rana Plaza factory building, the Government of Bangladesh, employers, trade unions and non-governmental organizations (NGOs) came together to form the Rana Plaza Coordination Committee (RPCC).

With the ILO acting as a neutral chair, the RPCC's purpose was to develop a compensation scheme that would deliver support to the victims, their families and dependants in a predictable manner consistent with relevant international labour standards.

The Rana Plaza Donors Trust Fund received contributions worth US$30 million from companies and individuals who wished to support financial and medical delivery to the Rana Plaza victims and their families (http://www.ranaplaza-arrangement.org).

The RPCC oversees the delivery of payments to the victims and their families and safeguards the fund against fraud. Benefits are calculated in a consistent manner, taking into account the standards of the International Labour Organization (ILO) and Bangladesh laws.

3. Weakness of the employers' liability programme in Bangladesh

The Bangladesh Labour Act stipulates employers' obligations to provide lump-sum compensation in cases of deaths or permanent disabilities resulting from work-related accidents.

However, this compensation scheme suffers from major shortcomings:

1. The compensation amounts under the Labour Act are paid in a lump sum and cannot guarantee lifetime income security for the injured workers or their dependents.
2. The compensation amounts under the Labour Act were also small and do not meet the minimum standards of the ILO's Employment Injury Benefits Convention, 1964 (No. 121). In Bangladesh, the compensation amount payable in case of death is equal to a lump-sum payment of 100,000 Bangladeshi Taka (BDT) and BDT125,000 in the case of permanent total disability. According to Convention No. 121, a widow aged 25 with two children (aged 3 and 5) should receive a periodical benefit equal to 50 per cent of the deceased worker's wage at the time of the accident. Calculating this at the minimum wage of BDT3,000 a month at the time of the accident, the total compensation would be at least BDT600,000.
3. Most of the employers went out of business after the Rana Plaza collapse. Due to their insolvency or bankruptcy, most employers did not have the financial means to pay the compensation amounts.

4. According to the Labour Act, only a limited list of injuries qualifies a victim to receive permanent total or partial disability status. Many Rana Plaza victims did not fall into these categories of injuries. For example, the following types of injuries are not covered by the Labour Act: spinal cord injuries, paralysed limbs, kidney malfunction, head trauma, back pain, psychological consequences and damage.

4. Towards a comprehensive Employment Injury Protection and Rehabilitation Scheme

In parallel to the Rana Plaza Compensation scheme, the Government of Bangladesh, led by the Ministry of Labour and Employment, has recognized the importance to set up a long-term, rights-based and sustainable protection mechanism that provides protection, as well as prevention and rehabilitation measures, in a systematic way.

Consequently, the Government signed a letter of intent with the ILO and the Government of Germany to explore the possibility of setting up of a national Employment Injury Protection & Rehabilitation (EIP&R) Scheme in line with the ILO Employment Injury Benefits Convention, 1964 (No. 121).

Following the key principles highlighted in the Convention, the national Employment Injury Protection & Rehabilitation Scheme (EIP&R) aims at providing protection in the forms of:
1. long-term periodical payments instead of lump-sum payments;
2. compensation for the loss of income over the lifetime of injured workers and dependents of deceased workers;
3. medical and associated care provided over the lifetime of severely injured workers; and
4. vocational rehabilitation programmes for reintegration of injured workers in their previous or alternative suitable occupation.

The proposed EIP&R scheme will provide the following advantages compared to the existing employers' liability:

1. It will provide adequate protection to workers and their families against the financial consequences of employment injuries.
2. It will guarantee access to health-care services as well as physical and vocational rehabilitation for injured workers.
3. Due to its collective risk-pooling mechanism, it will also protect employers against the financial consequences of catastrophic accidents.
4. The EII will not only guarantee the well-being of households, but at a macro level this will have a positive impact on aggregate demand for goods and services and the development of domestic markets.
5. The EII will also contribute to reduce risks of social unrest and promote social peace and stability that are conducive to the development of business.
6. The EII will finally reduce financial and reputational risks for brands and buyers that will no longer be responsible for compensating injured workers in factories.

5. What remains to be done?

The Rana Plaza catastrophe in April 2013 was a wake-up call for the industry and created momentum to improve the safety and health conditions and compensation mechanisms for workers, not only in Bangladesh but also around the world. The set-up of an employment injury scheme is a complex task that needs joint efforts and dialogues of all relevant stakeholders.

Good communication of the principles and design of the scheme with all stakeholders throughout the process is essential. Key principles, such as the importance of periodical payments of compensation, should be clearly explained.

In parallel with building the financial basis and administrative aspects of the scheme, it is important to drive the establishment of health and rehabilitation facilities and to ensure coverage in urban and rural areas. Return to work facilities and programmes, providing support to victims to re-enter the job market, are essential tools that enhance the effectiveness of the scheme.

Furthermore, setting incentives for different industries to reduce accidents and improve health and safety standards at work should receive adequate attention. Collection and management of statistical data and appropriate management information systems and clear operational procedures and guidelines are essential for the good governance of the future scheme and for improving operations.

6. References

ILO. 2014a. Workplace injury insurance must be part of the Rana Plaza legacy, speech by Gilbert Houngbo, ILO Deputy Director-General for Field Operations and Partnership. Available at: www.ilo.org/global/about-the-ilo/newsroom/news/WCMS_319637/lang--en/index.htm.

—. 2014b. World Social Protection Report 2014/2015 (Geneva). Available at: www.social-protection.org/gimi/gess/RessourcePDF.action?ressource.ressourceId=45417

—. 2015. Bangladesh – Rana Plaza Compensation Scheme: Technical report on the scheme design and operationalization, and lessons learnt (Geneva).

—. 2016. Introducing a National Employment Injury Protection and Rehabilitation Scheme for Bangladesh (Dhaka).

Rana Plaza Arrangement Coordination Committee. 2016. Rana Plaza Arrangement. Available at: http://ranaplaza-arrangement.org/.

2

Brazil: Bolsa Verde and Bolsa Floresta[5]

Brazil's invaluable rainforests have dwindled in recent decades as agriculture and other development have moved in. Development opportunities are crucial for many rural populations who continue to live in poverty. Now, the Government is attempting to address poverty and threats to the environment together through a new social protection programme.

Brazil is home to one of the largest stretches of tropical rainforest. However, persistent poverty in the country makes unsustainable economic opportunities attractive for many. In 2011, the Government began providing additional assistance designed to help the poor who reside in protected natural areas to engage in sustainable economic activities. The Bolsa Verde programme has now reached tens of thousands of beneficiaries. However, little is empirically known about its impacts on poverty and, moreover, the environment.

1. Main lessons learned

- The Amazonian rainforest represents a renewable, productive resource critical for reducing greenhouse gas in the atmosphere that is responsible for climate change. Only 80 per cent of the forest that existed in 1970 remains today, with the remainder under considerable threat from development pressures.

---

[5] This chapter was authored by James Canonge of the ILO and reviewed by Valérie Schmitt of the ILO. It was first published in September 2016.

- Despite progress, poverty persists, particularly in rural areas. The Bolsa Família cash transfer programme continues to address the worst forms of the country's poverty and provides an opportunity to address Brazil's environmental woes as well.
- Additional cash is now provided through Bolsa Verde to extremely poor families already participating in Bolsa Família. The programme also provides business and training opportunities for these households to engage in sustainable enterprise development, including latex extraction, artisanal fishing and handicraft production from natural resources.
- While over 50,000 extreme poor families in Brazil have received the additional benefits, the programme's net welfare effects, considering land use restrictions faced by beneficiaries and the ultimate impact on the environment, are less clear.

2. Brazil's forests are under threat

Forests play a vital role in stabilizing the environment and rolling back the causes of global climate change by absorbing carbon and reducing the presence of greenhouse gasses (GHG) in the atmosphere. For its part, the Amazon rainforest in Latin America is one of the world's largest swaths of natural forest, stretching from Peru in the west and to the coasts of French Guyana and Brazil in the east, and is estimated to store between 80 and 120 billion metric tons of carbon. The area of the Amazon represents more than half of the Earth's remaining rainforests, and roughly 60 per cent of the Amazon rainforest is located inside the country of Brazil.

For the world, the Amazon represents an important tool in the fight against climate change. It is estimated that if destroyed, some 50 times the annual GHG emissions of the United States could be released from former carbon sinks. For Brazil, the Amazon represents a huge ecological—but also economic—asset. While its value as a powerful carbon sequestration instrument is widely recognized, economic pressures have led to the development of Amazonian land, often at the expense of the natural flora.

Brazil's forests have suffered protracted, although recently slowed, losses.

Figure 1: Annual forest loss (in km²) and forest cover remaining in Brazil (per cent of 1970 cover)

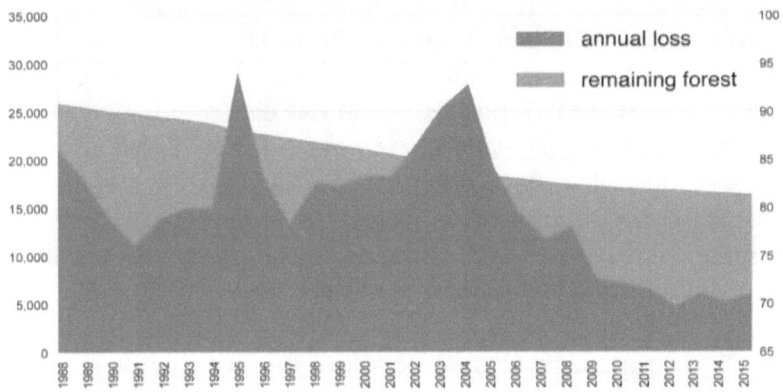

Source: Butler, R. Calculating Deforestation Figures for the Amazon (2016). Available at: http://rainforests.mongabay.com/amazon/deforestation_calculations. html.

Between 1970 and 2015, nearly 770,000 km2 of the Brazilian Amazon rainforest was lost to deforestation, primarily due to livestock, logging, and plantation-scale agricultural activities. According to several reports, roughly 80 per cent of lost rainforest lands are now occupied by cattle ranching, a sector dominated by medium and larger ranchers who possess almost 90 per cent of the land in the nine states that make up the Amazon basin. The Government has actively nurtured and subsidized cattle ranching activities for many years, and the sector is predicted to continue growing to satisfy an increasing global demand for beef. However, the most acute deforestation of the Amazon appears to be in the past, and, since 2004, the annual deforestation rate in the Brazilian Amazonia was reduced by 82 per cent between 2004 and 2014.

Brazil has often sought to clarify its role and that of other countries as custodians of ecological assets with implications for the wider global community. Brazil led the charge on incorporating environmental considerations into international development discussions in recent decades. In 1992, Brazil hosted the UN Conference on Environment and Development (UNCED), or Earth Summit, and the Rio+20 summit two decades later. It was a participant at the 2015 UN Climate Change Conference (COP 21) in Paris and in the discussions that led to the adoption of the Paris Agreement. In fact, Brazil cited its progress in rolling back deforestation and related greenhouse gas emissions as one of its primary commitments to combat climate change in its Intended Nationally Determined Contributions (INDCs) submitted to the COP 21.

3. The country has made considerable strides to combat extreme poverty

Brazil is the world's fifth most populous country, with more than 205 million people living within its borders. Historically, large swaths of Brazilian society have experienced chronic poverty, although the country's ascension to an upper-middle-income country and an expansion of anti-poverty programmes have helped to lift millions from poverty in recent decades. The extreme poverty rate (measured internationally as those living on less than US$1.25 per day) in Brazil has dropped from nearly 21 per cent in 1990 to under 5 per cent of the population in 2013.

One of the most widely known and studied anti-poverty programmes is a conditional cash transfer introduced in 2003 called Bolsa Família, which aims to lift people out of extreme poverty by combining cash transfers and increased access to public social services, including health and education. Bolsa Família reaches nearly 14 million participating households—

equivalent to roughly one quarter of the entire Brazilian population. The programme is income-tested and targets extremely poor households who report monthly incomes of less than 77 Brazil Reals (BRL) ($21) per person. As of January 2014, these households receive a monthly basic payment of BRL70 ($20), known as the "basic benefit", and are paid BRL32 ($9) per month for each child under 15 years and for each pregnant or breastfeeding mother. They also receive BRL38 ($10) per month for each adolescent between 16 and 17 years for a maximum of five children (or four children plus one mother) and two adolescents. Bolsa Família also targets households who are poor, but not extremely poor, who report living on less than BRL140 ($38) per person per month and who have children under the age of 18. These households receive the transfers for children, adolescents and mothers, but do not receive the basic benefit.

Extreme poverty in Brazil has fallen dramatically in recent decades.

Figure 2: Poverty headcount ratio at US$1.25 a day (PPP) in Brazil (per cent of population)

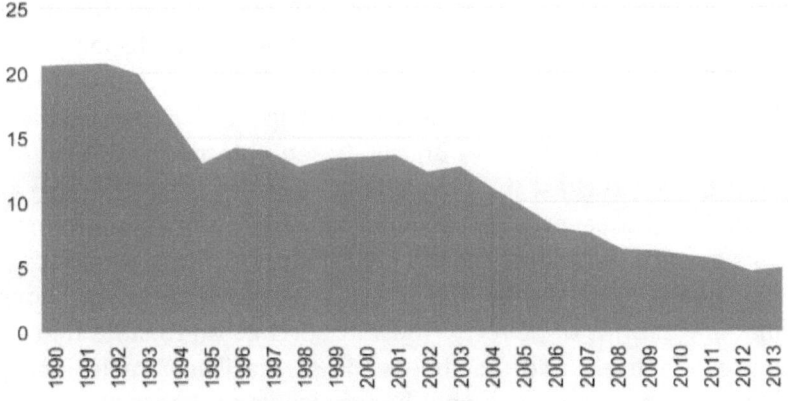

Source: World Development Indicators Database Archives (beta).

Participation in the programme is conditional, however. In order to receive the transfers, participating families must satisfy "co-responsibilities" seen as ways in which to develop the future earnings potential of participating households and ultimately supplying an exit strategy for families to graduate from Bolsa Família assistance over the long term. These responsibilities include pre- and post-natal health and nutrition monitoring, child immunizations and mandatory minimum school attendance by children.

Bolsa Família is jointly implemented at the federal and local levels. The federal bank, Caixa Econômica Federal, is in charge of central data administration and benefit payments. Approximately 5,500 municipalities implement Bolsa Família at the local level who are responsible for registering families and supplying information to monitor beneficiaries' fulfilment of the co-responsibilities. The programme uses a centralized, social registry called Cadastro Único, which, since its creation in 2001, has been the Government's main tool to identify poor populations and target them in anti-poverty initiatives. In 2013, Cadastro Único contained information on approximately 25 million Brazilian families.

According to the Government's own calculations, Bolsa Família can be credited for approximately 28 per cent of the total poverty reduction in Brazil since 2002, bringing the proportion of Brazilian society living on less than BRL70 ($20) per month down from 8.8 per cent to just 3.6 per cent in 2012. Other studies, such as one led by the Brasilia-based International Poverty Centre (IPC), suggest the programme has been more effective at reducing the severity of poverty in which many programme participants live, while having only limited success at reducing the number of those who live in extreme or even more moderate forms of poverty. These reports go on to state that to more effectively address the needs of Brazilian families living below the poverty line, higher benefit levels are needed.

4. **Through social protection, Brazil is aiming to address social and environmental needs together**

Building upon the successes of the Bolsa Família programme, the Government launched an additional cash grant in 2011 that sought to combine the anti-poverty function of Brazil's social protection system with the pressing need to protect the country's forests. The new programme, Bolsa Verde or "green grant", provides top-up transfers to extremely poor households already participating in Bolsa Família, almost half of whom live in rural areas. The programme links benefit payments to ecological or ecosystem services performed by beneficiaries. It joins a host of payment-for-ecosystem services (PES) operated in Brazil, although it is one of only two that effectively target marginalized populations. Bolsa Floresta is another conditioned payment made to "traditional and rural" residents across a number of geographic areas. In both programmes, participants are encouraged to develop sustainable economic activities, to maintain vegetation and conserve natural resources in the communities where they live.

As the only explicitly pro-poor programme, Bolsa Verde uses a means test for eligibility, the same test used by Bolsa Família for targeting households living in extreme poverty (defined as those living on less than BRL77 ($21) monthly per person). To be eligible, households must already receive the "basic benefit" from Bolsa Família and be registered with the Cadastro Único. Bolsa Verde participants must live in certain priority rural areas, many of which already have various restrictions that limit the scope or type of economic activities that can be conducted in the area.

Both Bolsa Família and Bolsa Verde provide benefits to extremely poor households in Brazil.

Figure 3: Monthly transfers by income group in Brazil (in Brazilian Reals)

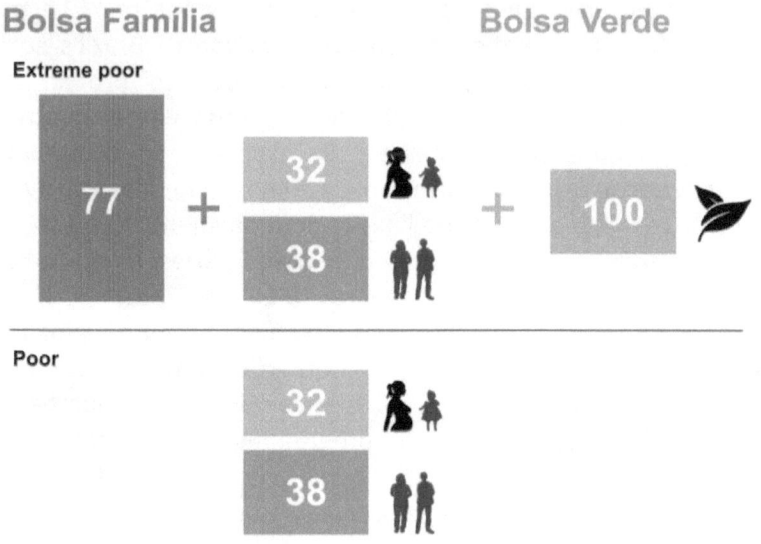

Note: Bolsa Verde payments are made quarterly (three times the monthly benefit).
Source: ILO, 2016, "Protecting people and the environment: Lessons learnt from Brazil's Bolsa Verde, China, Costa Rica, Ecuador, Mexico, South Africa and 56 other experiences."

Participating households receive BRL300 ($83) every three months for a period of up to two years. Families are allowed to use the resources provided by forests in a sustainable way. Among others, they are permitted to gather fruits, extract latex, conduct artisanal fishing and produce crafts from natural resources. The concrete rules for the sustainable use of natural resources and environmental conservation are established and described in the land management or regulation publications, which differ according to each priority area. A sample monitoring of beneficiary families is to be conducted periodically from 2014 onwards. However, indications of the poverty impacts or of the environmental performance of the programme have not yet been published. Bolsa Verde participation is supposed to include training for beneficiaries that offers assistance on production processes and marketing of ecologically-friendly products. As of January 2014, however, there was no information available on whether trainings had started.

The first phase was implemented in the nine Brazilian states in the *Amazônia Legal* (Legal Amazon), making up 61 per cent of the entire national territory. During a second stage that started in 2012, Bolsa Verde was expanded to the rest of the country. Of the 51,000 target households participating in the Bolsa Verde programme in 2014, 93 per cent lived in environmentally-protected areas, while the remaining 7 per cent lived in territories occupied by indigenous peoples. The large majority, if not all, of Bolsa Verde participants live in federally or otherwise protected areas with restrictions on land use. While the exact nature of the restrictions and the degree to which they limit the earnings potential of residents are so far unclear, the Bolsa Verde programme may serve to offset a portion of those anticipated losses and at the same time provides tools and incentives for residents to carry out more ecologically-friendly economic activities.

5. Little is known about poverty and climate impacts

As of January 2014, the Bolsa Verde programme had distributed cash to some 54,000 families, a welcome infusion of income for many of the country's ultra-poor. Undoubtedly, the top-ups to the modest Bolsa Família transfers are useful in addressing Brazil's most extreme instances of poverty. However, to date no ex post evaluation of Bolsa Verde has been conducted to provide more concrete figures on its impacts on poverty.

Monitoring of environmental upgrading or reforestation in target areas since the introduction of the Bolsa Verde programme also has yet to begin. When it does, it will be important for evaluators to distinguish between the incentivizing effects of Bolsa Verde from the punitive effects of the restrictions on land use in the areas where beneficiaries must live in order to participate in the programme.

Figure 4: ILO Guidelines for a "just transition"

In October 2015, a tripartite meeting of experts adopted a series of guidelines to ensure a just—or socially and economically equitable—transition towards greener economies and societies. Among the key policy areas covered in the guidelines is social protection. In particular, they suggest, "promot[ing] innovative social protection mechanisms that contribute to offsetting the impacts of climate change and the challenges of the transition on livelihoods, incomes and jobs."

These guidelines were adopted by the ILO's Governing Body in November 2015. The case of Brazil illustrates how the ILO guidelines can be applied and social protection policies used to ensure a "just transition."

Bolsa Verde and other payments tied to the performance of ecological services are some of the myriad anti-deforestation measures taken by the Brazilian government since the early 2000s. Measures include the clarification of land tenure, stepping up enforcement and compliance in protected areas and the development of "green" supply chains through, for example, revising government procurement rules to favour ecologically sourced products. The role that cash transfers play within the wider climate policy mix is likely marginal, although clearly further study is necessary.

These means-tested and geographically targeted transfers could represent important offsetting measures for residents in restricted-use areas whose livelihoods are potentially limited by pro-climate policies. As part of the "just transition" framework, Bolsa Verde appears to provide at least some compensation directed to low-income households in these areas to help them cope with the Government's climate adaptation policies and provide protection in the country's structural economic transition to more sustainable practices.

An increased focus on the development of tools could serve to provide the necessary framework and indicators to adequately and credibly measure the net welfare effects of the collection of environmental policies that affect rural residents in Brazil. Some limit earnings potential through land use restrictions while others provide new earnings opportunities through conservation activities. To assess the relevance and application of the ILO's own guidelines for a "just transition" and the provisions for offsetting social impacts of climate policies and climate change alluded to in the COP 21's outcome document, it will be necessary to evaluate the overall impact of positive and negative incentives used to engender a "greener" use of Brazil's forests, and examine the distribution of conservation responsibilities across the country's social strata.

6. References

Butler, R. 2016. "Calculating deforestation figures for the Amazon", Mongabay. Available at:
http://rainforests.mongabay.com/amazon/deforestation_calcul ations.html [2 Apr. 2016].

—. 2016, "People in the Amazon Rainforest", Mongabay. Available at:
http://rainforests.mongabay.com/amazon/amazon_people.html [2 Apr. 2016].

Government of Brazil; ILO. 2015. Brazil's contribution to the ILO's South-South and Triangular Cooperation Strategy: An overview, Brazil-ILO Annual South-South and Triangular Cooperation Meeting, Geneva, 10 June.

ILO. 2015. Outcome of the Tripartite Meeting of Experts on Sustainable Development, Decent Work and Green Jobs, Geneva, 5–9 Oct. (Geneva).

Pasolini, P. 2011. "Brazil launches program to help the poor engage in sustainable economy", Just Means. Available at: http://www.justmeans.com/blogs/brazil-launches-program-to-help-the-poor-engage-in-sustainable-economy [2 Apr. 2016].

Presentation by Andréa Arean Oncala, Manager, Bolsa Verde programme, Ministério do Meio Ambiente, Brasil.

Schwarzer, H.; van Panhuys, C.; Diekmann, K. 2016. Protecting people and the environment: Lessons learnt from Brazil's Bolsa Verde, China, Costa Rica, Ecuador, Mexico, South Africa and 56 other experiences, ESS – Working Paper No. 54 (Geneva, ILO).

3

China: Social protection in the face of climate change[6]

In China, there are big efforts to combat deforestation, with logging and other restrictions placed on large swaths of land. Nearly 1 million workers in state-owned forest enterprises who lost their jobs received help with job training and placement services. Other rural residents received cash to perform conservation activities.

China's forests are threatened by human activity, jeopardizing their ability to sequester carbon and combat soil erosion. A logging ban was enacted for the most threatened areas, laying off 1 million state forest workers. A new set of cash incentives were introduced to complement existing protections for workers. Large swaths of land were reforested, but welfare impacts for workers and residents in protected areas are largely unknown.

1. Main lessons learned

- China's forests are important for capturing carbon from the atmosphere and fighting soil erosion, but for decades, agricultural development and timber harvesting has destroyed this precious resource. Deadly floods linked to deforestation killed thousands in 1998.
- In 1998, the Government enacted a logging ban across newly protected lands. Nearly 1 million state forest

---

[6] This chapter was authored by James Canonge with contributions from Aidi Hu of the ILO and reviewed by Valérie Schmitt of the ILO. It was first published in September 2016.

workers were laid off. Another 120 million rural residents were also affected when the new restrictions on land use were put into place.

• New forest management opportunities, unemployment protections and state-led active labour market policies assisted many affected workers to find jobs elsewhere. Meanwhile, some 32 million rural households began receiving cash to perform conservation activities.

• In addition to protecting existing forests, 27 million hectares of agricultural and barren land were reforested. As China embarks on further ambitious economic restructuring schemes that impact the climate, more can be done to assess the projected and real impacts on workers and others affected by such policies.

2. China's invaluable forests are threatened by human activity

From the 1950s, China has experienced a considerable reduction in its otherwise rich and ecologically diverse forestlands. The forests serve several key environmental management functions, including the capture of carbon dioxide from the atmosphere and the prevention of soil erosion and flooding.

For decades, clear-cutting for agricultural development, timber harvesting and other human activities have destroyed much of the natural forests. This deforestation has led to severe soil erosion in the Yangtze and Yellow River basins, leaving the areas and its residents increasingly prone to flooding following heavy rains. From 1950 onwards, the incidence of natural disasters in the region increased, until in 1998 when a series of floods in the Yangtze River valley claimed the lives of over 3,000 people and resulted in more than 44 billion Yuan (CNY) (US$12 billion) in property damage and lost production.

The wooded watersheds of the Yangtze and Yellow Rivers also provide crucial carbon sinks that capture and sequester carbon dioxide (CO2) from the atmosphere, reducing greenhouse gasses and helping to roll back the effects of global climate change. In 1998, the Government began large-scale efforts to reforest certain areas of the Yangtze and Yellow River basins, along with other areas, to combat the soil erosion and resulting floods that threaten local communities.

The Government has also made reforestation one of the pillars of its efforts to reduce CO2 in the atmosphere and help mitigate climate change, as articulated in China's Intended Nationally Determined Contributions (INDCs) submitted to the 21st session of the Conference of the Parties (COP 21) to the United Nations Framework Convention on Climate Change (UNFCCC) in December 2015 in Paris. However, to rebuild considerable swaths of the country's forests, the Government took ambitious measures that affected millions of residents who rely on timber harvesting and processing and other forest activities to earn their livings.

3. An ambitious conservation action was adopted

Beginning in 1998, the Government imposed bans on logging in natural forests along the Yangtze River and Yellow River basins. As part of this plan, the Forest Conservation Program (FCP) was launched to provide incentives for individuals to comply with the ban and to reorganize the country's large publically-organized forestry industry to shift away from timber harvesting and processing towards forest management activities in those areas targeted for conservation.

At its launch, the FCP was ambitious in terms of the amount of land targeted for conservation. Its objective was to halt or reduce timber production by 2010 in the target areas, and conserve about 90 million hectares of existing natural forest. It also sought to reforest an additional 31 million hectares of then-barren but forest-suitable land through rejuvenation activities, including aerial seeding and manual planting of trees.

The FCP is administered by the State Forestry Administration. The initial pilot phase began in 12 provinces and autonomous regions in 1998. Between 1998 and 2000, some CNY22 billion ($3.4 billion) were allocated to the FCP by the State Council, allowing the addition of five more provinces to the programme before the year 2000. Another CNY96 billion ($14.8 billion) was committed by the State Council to finance the programme from 2000 to 2010.

In the most stringent of its provisions, the FCP banned all commercial logging in the Yangtze and Yellow River watershed areas in an effort to conserve over 61 million hectares of forest, bringing to a halt the regional production of more than 12 million cubic meters of annual timber harvest and processing.

Following new restrictions on logging, related employment in target provinces dropped.

Figure 5: Number of employed people in state-owned forestry enterprises in China's Heilongjiang province, 1997-2008

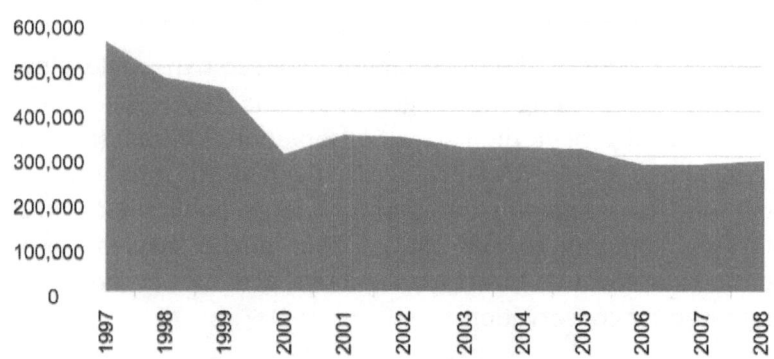

Source: Edstrom et al., 2012, "The Natural Forest Protection programme in China: A Contingent Valuation Study in Heilongjiang Province with data from China's Forest Statistical Yearbooks, 1997-2008."

Much of the FCP's financial resources were in the form of subsidies to state forest enterprises, designed to offset their revenue losses from reduced or halted timber production. Local governments also received funds from the central Government to help state forest enterprise workers who were laid off from their harvesting and processing jobs as a result of the restrictions. Across China, the number of people working in the forest enterprises dropped from almost 1 million in 1997 to just a quarter of that in 2010, affecting nearly 700,000 workers over the preceding decade. Meanwhile, a total 120 million local people, many of whom had previously carried out small-scale agriculture and other activities in newly protected forests, were affected by restrictions in the targeted rural areas.

4. Assistance was developed for affected workers and other residents

Some assistance to facilitate the move toward more sustainable economic activities in designated FCP areas was put into place for employees of the public forest companies and other affected rural residents. Much of the assistance took the shape of job placement services.

In 1998, the Government launched the Urban Employment and Reemployment Promotion Programmes (UERPP), which provides subsidies to social insurance contributions and other incentives for businesses to hire and for workers to undergo re-employment training.[7] Within the public forest sector, transfers were made possible largely by the creation of Forest Protection Units designed to manage the newly designated ecological forests. These units were then staffed by workers who had previously worked in the FCP areas in logging and related processing activities. In their new jobs that were salaried by the FCP, they worked to professionally conserve and replant the ecological forests. As part of the UERPP, recruitment offices were set up in the forest companies to help workers find other

---

[7] The Chinese welfare system has a historically dual structure with provisions typically falling into one of two categories: urban or rural. Employees of state-owned enterprises in China are eligible for "urban" benefit schemes, sometimes despite the location of their workplace.

local jobs, jobs in tourism, construction, or transportation, or jobs in the Eastern provinces where there were manufacturing opportunities, provided workers were willing to migrate to those areas. There was also support available for those wishing to start their own businesses.

For those in the labour force, workers in state-owned enterprises were enrolled in pension schemes for the "urban" working population. Once reaching pensionable age, they would begin to receive pension benefits from these schemes. Some who retired before reaching pensionable age could also take advantage of a lesser pension benefit paid directly by their former employer, or receive a lump-sum severance disbursement from their former employer. By 2002, four years following the inauguration of the logging ban, around two-thirds of affected workers had either been transferred to other jobs within the public forest sector, placed in jobs in other sectors of the economy or retired.

For those still unemployed and looking for work, as former employees of state-owned enterprises some unemployment protection benefits were available through the "urban" welfare system, which served to replace at least some of the protections workers had enjoyed during employment, including health insurance. The FCP provided some financial support to local governments to provide these benefits, as they were faced with severely increased demand following the logging bans and ensuing economic transformation, particularly in districts where the local economy had been heavily reliant upon forestry activity.

While the FCP articulated provisions for displaced workers and allotted resources to finance them, it did not include offsetting measures for other rural households. In fact, a total of 120 million rural residents were estimated to be affected by the new restrictions on logging in FCP target areas, but did not enjoy similar protections as workers of state-owned forest enterprises.

These residents were confronted with new restrictions on cutting firewood, conducting agricultural activities or performing other forest-related economic activities also prohibited by the FCP. This translated into increased tangible costs in terms of foregone crops, purchasing alternative energy sources and upgrading cooking and other equipment. For these residents, the Sloping Land Conversion Programme (SLCP) offered some offsetting support, although not without conditions.

From 1999 to 2002, a rice subsidy was the only form of compensation available through the SLCP. The amount of rice provided through the programme per household was often greater than the average household production, made possible by a crisis of grain supply that exceeded demand in the late 1990s, making SLCP participation attractive for many farming households. Surveys conducted on revenues from farming in SLCP provinces suggest that SLCP participation was actually more lucrative than farming for many households.[8]

Unlike the FCP, participation in the SLCP was, in theory, voluntary, provided participants lived in one of the 25 target provinces and were able to carry out conservation tasks like planting and nursing trees. However, many participants lived in areas with new restrictions on forest activities and more limited income-earning opportunities.

The Government provided 1.5 metric tonnes of rice per year for each hectare of cropland repurposed by programme participants for reforestation in the Yellow River watershed, and provided a higher subsidy of 2.25 metric tonnes of rice per year for each hectare in the Yangtze River watershed, where the agricultural production yields of farmers had typically been higher.

---

[8] According to surveys, in 1999, revenues from farming in Shaanxi province were CNY645 ($99) per hectare and CNY2,865 ($440) in Sichuan. Meanwhile, the value of rice subsidies received in these provinces was CNY2,400 ($369) and CNY3,450 ($530) per hectare, respectively.

Beginning in 2002, the Government introduced several complimentary cash compensation incentives, all of which were conditioned upon the performance of conservation activities. An additional CNY300 ($46) per hectare per year, known either as the "subsidy for living standard" or "education and medical subsidy", was introduced. The Government also began to provide CNY750 ($91) per hectare exclusively for the purchase of seeds and other supplies required to perform afforestation. (In some cases, these supplies are furnished in-kind by local authorities or by private companies if commercial bearing fruits or nuts trees are planted, provided that the harvest is sold back to the company.)

Grants were added to promote health and education and to offset seed purchases. Rice was entirely converted to cash in 2004.

Figure 6: SLCP transfers and values in China

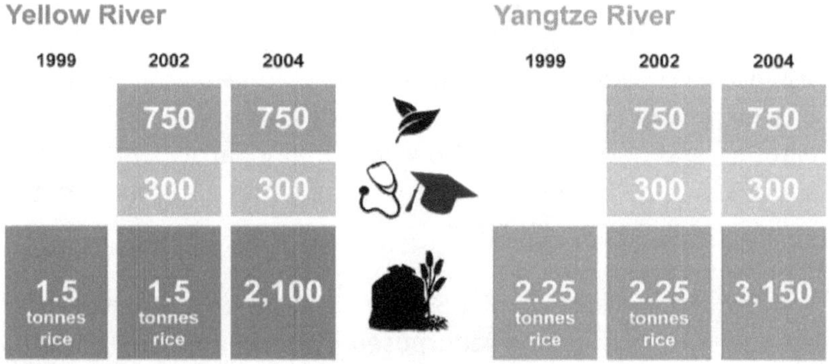

Note: Figures in Chinese Yuan unless otherwise indicated.
Source: Delang, C. O., W. Wang, 2013, "Chinese forest policy reforms after 1998: The case of the Natural Forest Protection Programme and the Slope Land Conversion Programme."

Since 2004, the remaining rice subsidy component was replaced entirely with an additional cash payment on top of the yearly CNY300 ($46) per hectare "subsidy for living standard" and seedling reimbursement schemes. Instead of the 1.5 metric tonnes of rice, participants received CNY2,100 ($322) per hectare of land reforested in the Yellow River watershed and approximately CNY3,150 ($483) in the Yangtze River watershed.

Depending upon the type of regeneration activity (conversion into grasslands, economically viable trees growing fruits or nuts or purely ecological trees), compensation lasted two, five or eight years, respectively. The compensation programme was initially slated to end in 2007. However, because of concerns over the viability of seedling forests and the continuing need for land management services by individuals, the programme was extended by another eight years, combining the minimum subsistence subsidy with a cash transfer of approximately half of what was previously paid, or CNY1,050 ($161) per hectare in the Yellow River watershed and CNY1,575 ($242) in the Yangtze watershed after 2007.

Empirically, programme participants were attracted in large numbers by the SLCP's food and cash incentives. Between 1999 and 2008, the SLCP involved 124 million people or 32 million households in reforestation and conservation activities.

Figure 4: ILO Guidelines for a "just transition"

In October 2015, a tripartite meeting of experts adopted a series of guidelines to ensure a just—or socially and economically equitable—transition towards greener economies and societies. Among the key policy areas covered in the guidelines is social protection. In particular, they suggest, "promot[ing] innovative social protection mechanisms that contribute to offsetting the impacts of climate change and the challenges of the transition on livelihoods, incomes and jobs."

These guidelines were adopted by the ILO's Governing Body in November 2015. The case of China illustrates how the ILO guidelines can be applied and social protection policies used to ensure a "just transition."

5. Impacts and way forward

Together, the FCP and SLCP programmes have contributed to the vast reforestation of agricultural or otherwise suitable barren land in China. Compared to its ambitions of conserving 90 million hectares of existing natural forest and reforesting 31 million hectares of additional land, the country was able to reforest nearly 27 million hectares of former farmland and deforested areas as part of its efforts—a massive reversal of the rapid deforestation experienced over prior decades.

Protections extended to affected workers were in part made possible thanks to China's public organization of its timber harvesting and processing sectors, as well as the ensuing forest management industry that sprung up following the inauguration of the FCP. China's state-owned enterprises employ roughly half of the country's 750 million strong workforce. This has allowed the Government to use tools that others cannot in order to offset the employment impacts of some of its recent economic and environmental reforms. However, as the share of gross domestic product to which state-owned enterprises contribute shrinks (representing around 80 per cent of China's GDP in 1979 versus just 18 per cent in 2012), other mechanisms will play an increasingly large role in providing support to workers affected by environmental policies.

The transition was also facilitated by China's existing unemployment and other social protection provisions, which provided unemployment benefits, re-employment services, pensions, social welfare and other support to workers affected by the conservation effort.

China's social protection system will be instrumental moving forward as the country takes aim at other sectors of the economy in its efforts to address rampant air pollution and other environmental problems.

Following the COP 21 hosted in Paris, the Government announced in January 2016 a moratorium on new coal mining permits and announced plans to close roughly 4,300 existing mines in the years ahead. In February, the Government also announced a financial commitment of some CNY100 billion ($15.3 billion) to support an estimated 1.8 million workers affected by planned structural reforms in both the coal mining and steel production sectors, an equivalent of roughly CNY56,000 ($8,500) per affected worker. Provisions similar to those used for FCP-affected employees are envisaged, including subsidies for enterprises to create new jobs for laid-off workers, employment placement and training services, early retirement arrangements and public works programmes.

The Government has also announced intentions to continue its fight against climate change with a pledge of nearly 7 per cent of the 2014 public budget, CNY138 billion ($23 billion), to support climate change adaptation and mitigation efforts, including more conservation efforts and returning farmland to forests.

Moving forward, it would be useful to develop the tools necessary to measure the net welfare effects of many of these policies that, on the one hand, limit earnings potential through land use restrictions and, on the other, provide new earning opportunities for conservation activities. Such resources will be needed to assess the relevance and application of the ILO's own guidelines for a "just transition" and the provisions for offsetting social impacts of climate policies and climate change effects alluded to in the COP 21 outcome document, or the "Paris Agreement", which recognizes that innovative mechanisms will be needed to offset inevitable "loss and damage" resulting from both climate change itself and states', including China's, efforts to address it.

6. References

Cao, S.; Wang, X.; Song, Y.; Chen, L.; Feng, Q. 2010. "Impacts of the Natural Forest Conservation Program on the livelihoods of residents of North-western China: Perceptions of residents affected by the program", in Ecological Economics, Vol. 69, No. 7, pp. 1454–1462.

Carter, J.; Bédard, C.; Bista, C.P. 2013. Comparative review of unemployment and employment insurance experiences in Asia and worldwide(Bangkok, ILO).

Delang, C.O.; Wang, W. 2013. "Chinese forest policy reforms after 1998: The case of the Natural Forest Protection Program and the Slope Land Conversion Program" in International Forestry Review, Vol. 15, No. 3, pp. 290-304.

Edström, F.; Nilsson, H.; Stage, J. 2012. "The Natural Forest Protection Program in China: A Contingent Valuation Study in Heilongjiang Province with data from China's Forest Statistical Yearbooks, 1997-2008", in Journal of Environmental Science and Engineering, Vol. 1, pp. 426-432.

ILO. 2015a. Outcome of the Tripartite Meeting of Experts on Sustainable Development, Decent Work and Green Jobs, Geneva 5-9 Oct. (Geneva).

—. 2015b. "Universal pension coverage: People's Republic of China" in Social Protection in Action: Building Social Protection Floors (Geneva).

Xu, J.; Yin, R.; Li, Z.; Liu, C. 2006. "China's ecological rehabilitation: Unprecedented efforts, dramatic impacts, and requisite policies" in Ecological Economics, Vol. 57 No. 4, pp. 595-607.

Yuexian, Y. 2001. "People's Republic of China", in P.B. Durst et al. (eds): Forests out of bounds: Impacts and effectiveness of logging bans in natural forests in Asia-Pacific (Bangkok, FAO).

4

China: Social protection for rural migrants[9]

More than 270 million people, accounting for 35 per cent of the national labour force, have migrated from their rural villages to urban cities in China. Due to a series of expansionary measures of the social protection system in China – particularly the expansion of the minimum living standard guarantee (Dibao) to all rural and urban poor and the introduction of subsidized health insurance and pension schemes for urban and rural residents – the social protection coverage of rural migrant workers has significantly improved in recent years. More rural migrant workers are also progressively included under the social insurance for urban workers, which provides them with more comprehensive and higher levels of protection.

1. Main lessons learned

- China's experience shows that migrant workers, despite their large number and high mobility, can progressively be included under existing social protection schemes.
- Extensive coverage of the migrants was feasible because of large government subsidies for those without formal jobs or self-employed.
- Thanks to the Social Security Law enacted in 2010 that requires rural migrant workers to affiliate under the social insurance scheme for urban workers, and the introduction of health and pension schemes for urban

---

[9] This chapter was authored by Aidi Hu of the ILO and reviewed by Isabel Ortiz and Valérie Schmitt of the ILO. It was first published in September 2016.

and rural residents in which many rural migrant workers participated together with their rural or urban-based families, migrant workers and their families are better integrated into urban life with higher levels of consumption and improved health status, all of which are essential for achieving a harmonious society, which is a national strategic objective.

• However, the achievement of basic and universal coverage is only the first step. As China develops, continuous efforts are needed to improve the adequacy of protection for migrant workers.

Figure 7: Structure of China's social insurance system[10]

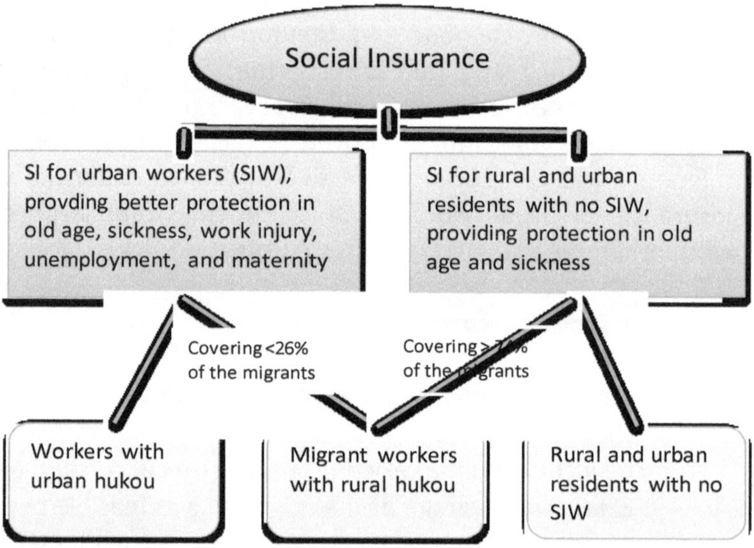

Social Insurance

SI for urban workers (SIW), provding better protection in old age, sickness, work injury, unemployment, and maternity

SI for rural and urban residents with no SIW, providing protection in old age and sickness

Covering <26% of the migrants

Covering >74% of the migrants

Workers with urban hukou

Migrant workers with rural hukou

Rural and urban residents with no SIW

2. How are migrants covered?

In China, social protection was extended to rural migrant workers through two main schemes: health insurance and old-

[10] A hukou is a record in a government system of household registration which determines where citizens are allowed to live.

age pension schemes for rural or urban residents (SIR) and the Social Insurance for urban Workers (SIW).

Urban workers are registered under the SIW, while rural and urban residents are entitled to the SIR, which offers a lower level of protection compared to the SIW. Initially, most of rural migrant workers were covered by the SIR. However, the new Social Security Law enacted in 2010 authorizes rural migrant workers working in urban areas to be registered by their employers under the SIW.

As a result of the implementation of the Social Security Law, the number of migrant workers participating in SIW has increased in the last few years. Today, the proportion of rural migrant workers covered by the SIW has reached 26 per cent of the total number of rural migrant workers.

Figure 8: Insured migrant workers under the SIW in China (in millions), 2006-14

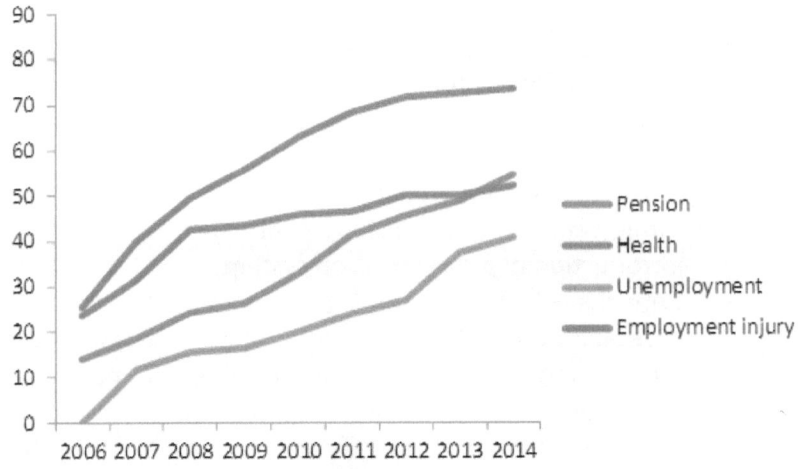

Source: SB 2006-14.

As a result of the inclusion of rural migrant workers in the SIR and SIW and the extension of coverage under these two schemes, today rural migrant workers are better protected. Out of the 277 million rural migrant workers in 2015, around 80 per cent were covered by the old-age pension schemes either for urban workers or for residents, and over 95 per cent were covered by health insurance schemes either for urban workers or for residents. In addition, all poor rural migrant workers are entitled to a minimum living standard guarantee called Dibao. The objective of the Government is to provide basic health and pension protection to the entire population, including this group, by 2020.

3. How were these breakthroughs achieved?

The effective extension of social protection to rural migrant workers can be explained by a number of national and regional policies and initiatives.

- At the national level, the Central Committee of the Community Party of China (CC of CPC) and the State Council decided in 2002 to strengthen rural health. This lead to the creation of a rural health insurance programme in 2003.
- The State Council decided in 2007 to extend the minimum living standard guarantee (Dibao) to rural residents; it provides income security and other social assistance services to the rural poor.
- The CC of CPC adopted a policy in 2009 concerned with rural reform and development that led to the introduction of a rural pension system.
- With the adoption of the Social Insurance Law in 2010, coverage under SIW for all rural migrant workers with employment contracts became a legal requirement.
- In line with the Social Insurance Law, the Employment Injury Regulation was revised in 2011. This has facilitated the extension of employment injury insurance to migrant workers and it now has the highest coverage rate within all branches of SIW.
- A government policy was adopted in 2013 to gradually merge the urban and rural residents' health insurance

programmes. Although the merge has yet to be completed, the schemes' essential parameters, such as benefit packages and fiscal subsidies, are being aligned and strengthened.

- The State Council decided in 2014 to merge the basic old-age insurance programmes for urban and rural residents. Measures on improving the portability of accumulated social security rights and entitlements were developed and implemented. Migrant workers today are better protected, which encourages more workers to migrate within China.

Another important feature of the Chinese social protection system is decentralization. Local authorities are responsible for the design and daily management of their schemes in line with the principles set by the central Government. The level of regional motivation, commitment and innovation is thus as important as the national policies in the extension of social protection coverage to rural migrant workers. Shanghai can be presented here as a concrete example.

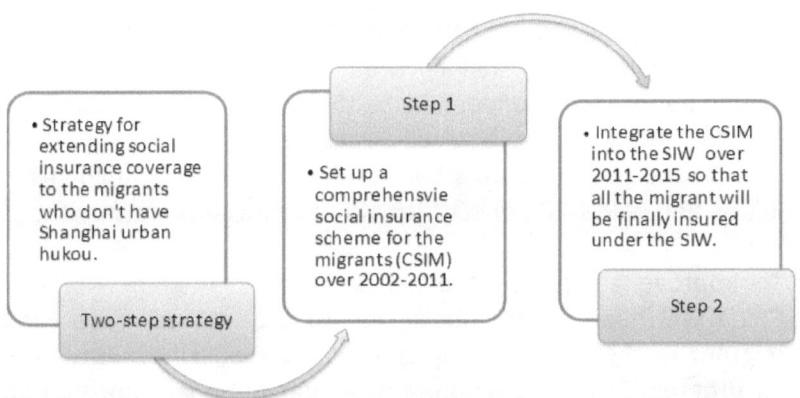

The metropolitan government of Shanghai was innovative in its strategy to extend SIW coverage to migrants. Extension started with a transitional scheme called Comprehensive Social Insurance for Migrants (CSIM). Instead of providing the insured migrants a full range of social insurance, CSIM focused on protection in three branches, namely employment injury, hospitalization and retirement. After nine years of operation, more and accurate information had been collected, administrative capacity strengthened and the coverage of CSIM broadened. In 2011 the metropolitan government of Shanghai launched the second step, i.e. integrating CSIM into the mainstream SIW scheme.

It is expected that when the integration is complete, more rural migrant workers employed in the region of Shanghai (regardless their type of hukou) will be covered under SIW than urban workers. This will contribute to increasing the adequacy of benefit entitlements for rural migrant workers.

4. What are the remaining challenges?

As explained previously, SIW provides higher levels of protection compared to SIR. SIR, for instance, does not provide any protection in the case of work injury, unemployment and maternity.

Despite the enactment of the Social Security Law in 2010, most migrant workers are still covered by SIR even though they should be registered under SIW by their employers. As indicated on the graph below, SIW coverage rates of those working outside their rural town is below 30 per cent for employment injury, and below 20 per cent for old-age pensions and health.

To improve adequacy of benefits for rural migrant workers, China will need to provide access to the SIW to more rural migrant workers by fully implementing the Social Security Law. To progress in this direction, a four-year national campaign on universal social security registration was launched by the Ministry of Human Resources and Social Security (MOHRSS) in 2014. The campaign aims to develop an integrated national social security database so that full coverage, particularly for vulnerable groups like rural migrant workers, can be progressively achieved.

Figure 9: Coverage rates of those working outside their rural town in China (per cent)

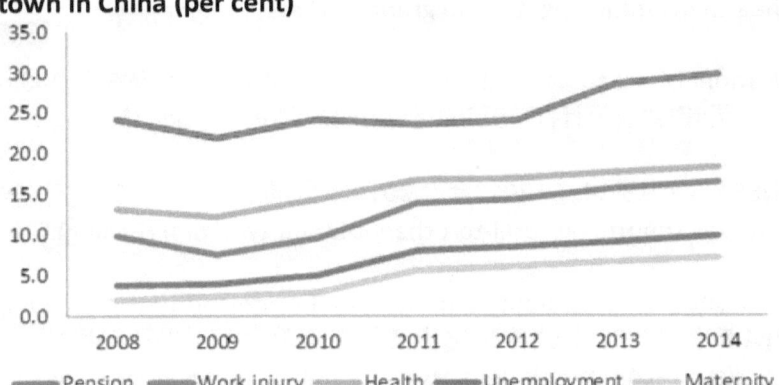

Source: National survey report on rural-to-urban migrant workers, 2013 and 2014.

5. References

Central Committee of the Communist Party of China (CC of the CPC) and State Council. 2002. 中共中央、国务院关于进一步加强农村卫生工作的决定 [Joint decision on further strengthening the rural health service] (Beijing).

CC of the CPC. 2008. 中共中央关于推进农村改革发展若干重大问题的决定 [Decision on facilitating rural reform and development] (Beijing).

Huang, H. 2015. 中国医保与农民工医疗保障 [Health protection of migrant workers], presented at a seminar organized by ILO and All China Federation of Trade Unions of the Peoples' Republic of China (P.R.C.) (ACFTU) (Kunming).

Ministry of Human Resource and Social Security of the P.R.C (MOHSS). 2006-14. 历年人力资源和社会保障事业发展统计公报 [Annual Statistics Bulletins on the Development of Human Resources and Social Security] (Beijing).

MOHRSS. 2011. 流动就业人员基本医疗保障关系转移接续暂行办法 [Provisional measures on transfer and maintenance of health insurance rights of migrant workers] (Beijing).

National Bureau of Statistics of China of the P.R.C (NBS). 2005-14. 历年中国统计年鉴 [China Statistical Yearbooks] (Beijing).

NBS. 2013-14. 2013年、2014年全国农民工监测调查报告 [Survey reports on rural-to-urban migrant workers] (Beijing).

National Development and Reform Commission of the P.R.C (NDRC). 2013. 发改委：逐步统一城乡居民基本医疗保险制度 [Policy recommendations on gradually unifying the health insurance schemes for urban and rural residents] (Beijing).

Peoples' Congress of the P.R.C. 2010. 社会保险法 [Social Insurance Law] (Beijing).

Social Security Net. 2014. 人社部将启动全民参保登记计划 [A universal social security registration program to be launched by MOHRSS] (Beijing).

Shanghai bureau of the ACFTU. 2015. 着力保障农民工平等享有社会保险权益 [Protecting the equal social insurance rights of migrant workers], presented at a seminar which was organized jointly by the ILO and ACFTU (Kunming).

State Council. 2007. 国务院关于在全国建立农村最低生活保障制度的通知 [Circular No. 19 of 2007 concerning the setting up of the MLSG program for the rural population] (Beijing).

State Council. 2011. 工伤保险条例 [Employment Injury Insurance Regulation] (Beijing).

State Council. 2014. 国务院关于建立统一的城乡居民基本养老保险制度的意见 [Decision on developing a unified pension system for all urban and rural residents] (Beijing).

5

El Salvador: Universal social protection[11]

Recently, El Salvador has taken firm steps to establish a universal social protection system. The Government's strong political commitment and social dialogue have contributed significantly to this process.

The Universal Social Protection System introduced in 2009 ensures universal social protection in the areas of health, food, income security, and vocational training. In 2014, the Congress adopted the Development and Social Protection Act, in order to institutionalize the Universal Social Protection System and enhancing its operation.

These initiatives are transforming the structure of the social protection system in El Salvador with an impressive socio-economic impact. Between 2008 and 2012, poverty rates fell from 39.9 to 34.5 per cent, while inequality, measured by means of the Gini index, dropped from 0.48 to 0.41.

1. Main lessons learned

- Investment in social protection is a reliable way to reduce inequality, as shown by the positive impact on the Gini index in El Salvador.

---

[11] This chapter was authored by Fabio Durán-Valverde and José Francisco Ortiz-Vindas of the ILO and reviewed by Isabel Ortiz, Helmut Schwarzer and Valérie Schmitt of the ILO. It was first published in August 2015.

- Linking social programmes to productive development, for example, by including micro-enterprises as suppliers in social protection programmes, generates positive effects on local economies.
- The experience of El Salvador's Universal Social Protection System shows that social dialogue is essential to implement political agreements aimed at increasing and maintaining social expenditures.
- The rights-based approach adopted by El Salvador is an essential element to support universal policies for social protection.
- Mainstreaming social protection strategies, programmes, and processes through developing a legal framework supports and ensures their continuity. A good example is the enactment of the Development and Social Protection Act in El Salvador.

2. What does the system look like?

Social protection in El Salvador is structured through its Universal Social Protection System (USPS). The USPS is guided by rights-based principles and by a strategy based on a life-cycle approach, with a focus on gender equality. The system includes non-contributory universal interventions, which ensure a social protection floor for the whole population, and is complemented by contributory components.

The Technical Secretariat of the Presidency (TSP) is responsible for coordinating the system and a number of institutions and ministries take part in its implementation.

Benefits. Although the USPS follows a universalist approach, the non-contributory components are mainly targeted at persons who are socially vulnerable. Caring Communities (urban and rural) is considered to be the main programme and involves interventions for specific age groups. For example, the School Kits programme targets children; the Temporary Income Support programme targets working-age individuals; and Our Senior

Rights programme targets the elderly. The non-contributory component also includes universal health care provided through the Ministry of Health. In addition, social security provides contributory coverage to 25 per cent of the population.

Figure 10: El Salvador's Universal Social Protection System (USPS): non-contributory components

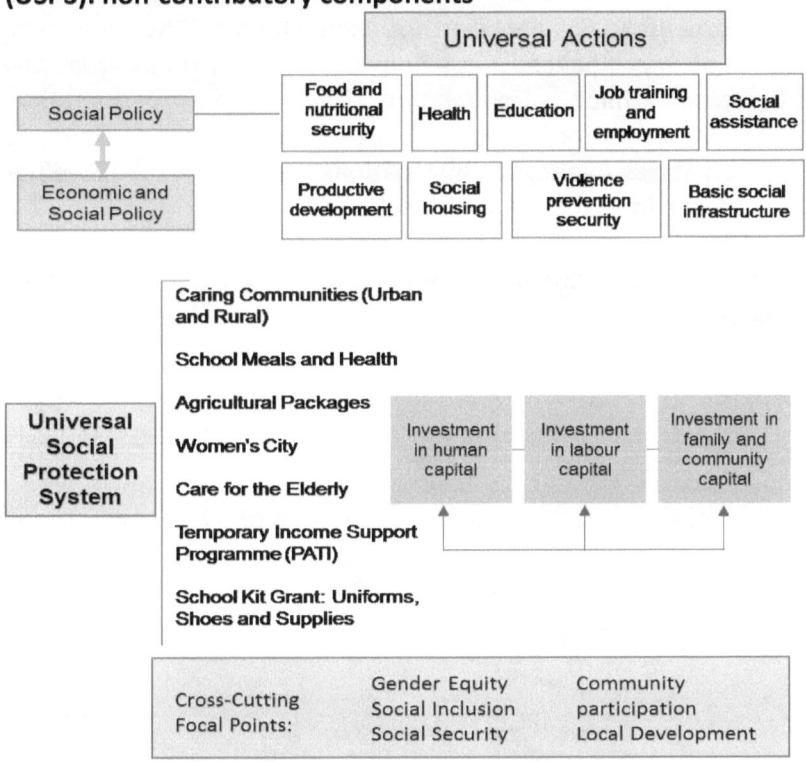

Source: STP, 2013.

Contributory programmes are organized through Social Insurance and a private pension scheme. Contributory coverage encompasses medical care, sickness and maternity, and compensation benefits for accidents at work and occupational diseases. Since 1998, disability, old age, and survivors' benefits have been administrated by the Pension Savings System, a system based on individual accounts and handled by private pension fund administrators.

Financing: Since the introduction of the USPS, El Salvador has made an unprecedented number of social investments. It is estimated that in 2013, expenditures on non-contributory transfers reached an amount equivalent to 0.7 per cent of GDP.

Between 2011 and 2013, the Government financed approximately 65 per cent of expenditures. The remaining amount was financed with non-reimbursable funds from the European Union, Luxembourg Development Cooperation, Spanish Agency for International Development Cooperation, and United States Agency for International Development, as well as with loans from the IDB and the World Bank.

Figure 11: Social transfer expenditure in El Salvador (% of GDP), 2006-13

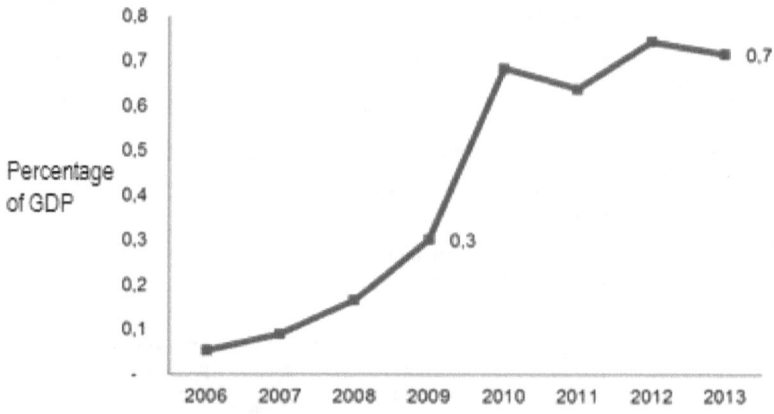

Source: Quiñonez (2014).

Legal aspects: The enactment of the Development and Social Protection Act in April 2014 provides legal support for the mainstreaming and consolidation of the USPS, as well as establishes conditions for the continuity of its principal interventions.

Benefits delivery: The coordination of the system is centralized and its management is decentralized. The Social Investment

Fund for Local Development, the Social Inclusion Secretariat, and several ministries, including Agriculture and Livestock, Education, and Labour and Social Security, implement the system. The USPS has three principal management tools: the Single Registry of Participants, the Social Programmes Information System, and the Social Policy Monitoring and Evaluation System.

3. How was this significant progress achieved?

Although the Government has been strongly committed to the expansion of social protection, the process of creating a new social protection system has not been easy. It is only recently that the Government has adopted an active social policy oriented towards developing universal social protection and establishing appropriate priorities. The principal interventions that have contributed to the process are: the creation of the USPS (2009); the Five-Year National Development Plan (2010-2014), which includes and prioritizes social protection; the Global Anti-Crisis Plan (2009); the reform of the health sector initiated in 2010, with the purpose of enhancing stewardship, health services, health-care staff and public participation; and the adoption of the Development and Social Protection Act (2014).

4. What are the main results?

According to the TSP, over 2 million people have benefited from the USPS since 2009 – equivalent to 30 per cent of the population. In 2013, the USPS invested over 183 US Dollars (US$) million in non-contributory benefits (TSP and ILO, 2013). In that year, the School Meals and Health Programme benefited over 1.4 million children; the Temporary Income Support Programme benefited close to 17,000 people; and the Universal Basic Pensions Programme covered close to 29,000 elderly persons. Out of a total of 262 municipalities nationwide, the Caring Communities Programme benefited 125 of them, with 100 of the municipalities being rural communities.

Since 2009, El Salvador has attached great significance to using social policy as a means to distribute and redistribute wealth, affecting poverty, inclusion, and equity. The country has witnessed the progressive decline of poverty and income inequality. Poverty rates fell from 39.9 per cent in 2008, to 34.5 per cent in 2012. Inequality, measured by means of the Gini index, dropped from 0.48 to 0.41 during the same period.

Figure 12: Gini index for El Salvador, 2004-12

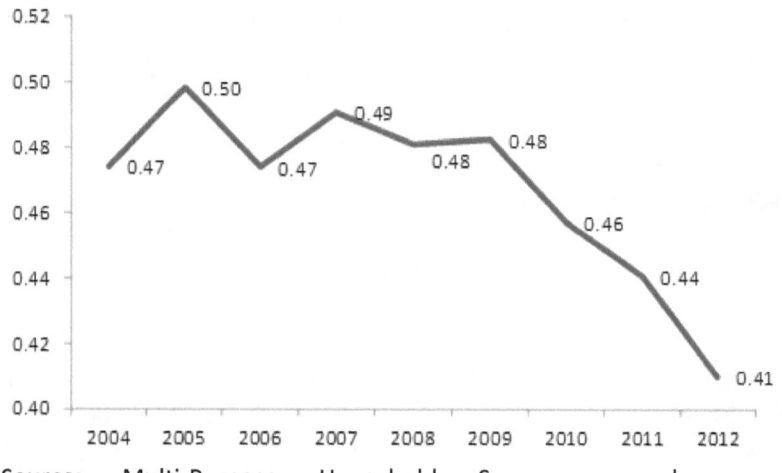

Source: Multi-Purpose Household Survey, several years. MINEC/DIGESTYC.

In El Salvador, social programmes generate productive chains and impact other sectors of the economy, with emphasis on strengthening local economies.

Some of the programmes have placed a priority on the mobilization of local micro-enterprises as providers of school supplies, uniforms, and food products. It is estimated that since 2009, the School Kits Programme has generated over 47,000 jobs and hired close to 4,300 suppliers, many of them from local communities. Through its Glass of Milk programme, the School Meals and Health programme has contracted approximately

2,200 cattle farmers as suppliers and it is expected that numbers will increase to 4,000 over the next few years.

5. What are the next steps?

Recent developments in the social protection system show unprecedented outcomes. However, a few challenges yet remain:

- Achieving greater linkages between the USPS and social policy in general, and improving coordination between institutions in the social sector.
- Expanding the fiscal space and, in particular, reducing external funding of programmes in order to make the system sustainable.
- Extending non-contributory programmes to additional highly vulnerable regions.
- Extending social security coverage to groups that are not covered, with the informal economy as a priority.
- Consolidating the health reform process under the leadership of the Ministry of Health.
- Strengthening and mainstreaming social dialogue instruments.

6. References

Asamblea Legislativa de El Salvador. 2014. Ley de Desarrollo y Protección Social. Decreto 647. (San Salvador). Available at: www.asamblea.gob.sv/eparlamento/indice-legislativo/buscador-de-documentos-legislativos/ley-de-desarrollo-y-protecion-social.

ILO. 2014. World social protection report 2014/2015. Building economic recovery, inclusive development and social justice (Geneva). Available at: www.social-protection.org/gimi/gess/ShowTheme.action?th.themeId=10.

—; Technical Secretariat of the Presidency. 2014. Revisión del gasto y desempeño de la protección social en El Salvador, 2013 (San Salvador).

Martínez, Juliana. 2013. Sistemas de protección social en América Latina y el Caribe: El Salvador (ECLAC). Available at: www.cepal.org/publicaciones/xml/2/49092/SPS_ElSalvador_esp .pdf.

Mesa-Lago, Carmelo; De Franco, Mario. 2010. Estudio sobre la protección social en Centroamérica Volumen 1. Available at: http://eeas.europa.eu/delegations/el_salvador/documents/mor e_info/estudio_sobre_la_proteccion_social_en_centroamerica_i nforme_general_volumen_1_es.pdf.

Miranda Baires, Danilo. 2014. Hacia un sistema de protección social universal en El Salvador: Seguimiento de un proceso de construcción de consensos (ECLAC). Available at: www.cepal.org/publicaciones/xml/5/53335/Haciaunsistemadep roteccionESal.pdf.

Quiñonez, Leslie. 2014. Políticas sociales y Sistema de Protección Social Universal. Con enfoque de derechos y ciclo de vida Presented at Taller Internacional de Primera Infancia y Protección Social, San Salvador, 19 Mar.

Technical Secretariat of the Presidency. 2013. Sistema de protección social universal (SPSU): Resumen ejecutivo (San Salvador). Available at: www.proteccionsocial.gob.sv/index/index.php/actualidad/boleti nes/finish/3-sistema-de-proteccion-social-universal/17-resumen-ejecutivo-sistema-de-proteccion-social-universal.

6

France: Active Solidarity Income[12]

The Active Solidarity Income (Revenu de Solidarité Active in French) provides a minimum income and measures aimed at supporting employability and return to work for the working poor and unemployed who receive insufficient income replacement.

In France, about 14 per cent of the population lives below the poverty line. Among this poor population, more than 50 per cent are people of working age, unemployed, or working poor (Observatoire des inégalités, 2014).

The social protection system in the past suffered from gaps leaving a share of the active age population without income security in case of long-term unemployment or poverty. In addition, many of the existing income support schemes did not provide sufficient incentives to facilitate return to work.

The creation of the Active Solidarity Income in 2008 had a twofold objective: ensuring access to universal income security for the active age population coupled with placement services and skills development, and generating incentives for return to work.

---

[12] This chapter was authored by Thibault van Langenhove and Clara van Panhuys of the ILO and reviewed by Valérie Schmitt and Christina Behrendt of the ILO, and Martin Hirsch of the Assistance publique – Hôpitaux de Paris. It was first published in November 2015.

1. Main lessons learned

- The Active Solidarity Income (RSA in French) is a programme for the unemployed and the working poor that has successfully managed to link social protection benefits and active labour market policies to support effective job-search efforts, employability, and reduce and eliminate financial disincentives to return to work.
- Evaluation reports show that concerns about employers using the RSA strategically to decrease wages or impose part-time jobs were not confirmed.
- The RSA is a concrete policy example that addresses poverty of the working poor in addition to providing income security for the unemployed.
- The RSA programme is too complex to be understood by potential beneficiaries and even some local staff in charge of its administration, which has negatively impacted its expansion and does not allow the scheme to achieve its intended goals.
- Also, there is a perceived stigma of poverty among some RSA beneficiaries. This is an important concern that should be taken into consideration when designing, implementing, and communicating about social policies and programmes.

2. What led to the creation of the RSA?

Prior to 2008, three means-tested benefits provided income security to the non-active working age population living in France: the Minimum Subsistence Income, the Single Parent Allowance, and the Specific Solidarity Allowance. These income transfers were not combined with any measures to facilitate return to work. Also, the benefits would be significantly reduced or halted when beneficiaries found jobs or started working longer hours. Thus, individuals found in some cases that they faced significant reductions in their total income as a result of returning to work or working more hours. These benefits in some cases discouraged work and led to so-called "inactivity traps", i.e. a vicious circle of inactivity and poverty. The programmes were also believed to have contributed to the expansion of undeclared work.

Negotiations organized in 2007-08 between the Government and social partners resulted in a national reform strategy aimed at simplifying and coordinating social inclusion programmes and linking them with active labour market policies. The strategy recommended a new social paradigm and the creation of the RSA.

The RSA was enacted by Law No. 2008-1249 of 1 December 2008. It is also included in the revised Social Action and Family Code of the 1 of June 2009.

3. How does the programme function?

The RSA aims to support households with insufficient incomes. Potentially eligible are adults above the age of 25, or under the age of 25 years if pregnant or with one or more dependents, or having worked at least two years during the last three years. French and European Union (EU) nationals should be legally residing in France for at least three months and non-EU nationals for five years. The programme targets unemployed persons (without work but available for work and seeking work) who receive insufficient income replacement, as well as the working poor.

The RSA income support is composed of two elements: the "Floor RSA" that is financed by local governments (Départements) guarantees a minimum income threshold, and the "Activity RSA" financed by the central Government is intended to create a work incentive.

Table 1: Floor RSA amounts in France, 2015

No. of children	Single person / parent	Couple
0	€483.24	€724.86
1	€724.86	€869.83
2	€869.83	€1,014.84
Additional children	€193.30	€193.30

Source: http://rsa-revenu-de-solidarite-active.com/montant-rsa/216-montant-rsa-2015.html.

The Floor RSA amount varies according to the household composition and is indexed on inflation (revised annually). The Floor RSA is the amount received when no member of the household is working.

Figure 13: Monthly guaranteed income according to the household monthly income from work for France's RSA – Simulation for a single person with one child assuming that no other social transfer is received.

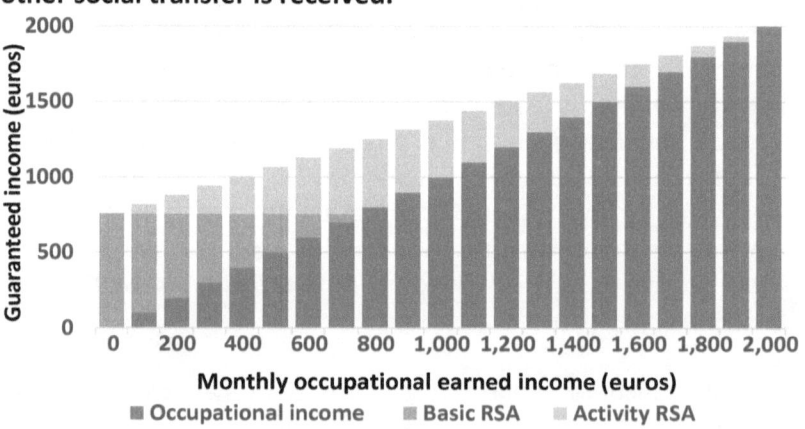

Source:
wwwd.caf.fr/wps/portal/caffr/aidesetservices/lesservicesenligne/esti mervosdroits/lersa

When the recipient works, even part time, the Floor RSA is reduced and an Activity RSA is added on to ensure that the total income (composed of Floor RSA, Activity RSA, and earnings) equals the Minimum Income Guarantee (MIG). This MIG is the Floor RSA plus 62 per cent of the earnings up to a threshold that is approximately the minimum wage for a single person.

The sum of all social transfers and earnings cannot exceed the MIG. Therefore, revenues that derive from other income support programmes (unemployment allowance, housing benefit, among others) are deducted from the RSA amount.

RSA beneficiaries have on principle the obligation to look for a job or take action to create their own enterprise. They receive support and placement advisory services, as well as training.

In 2014, total expenditure on RSA benefits represented 0.4 per cent of GDP (Observatoire national de l'action sociale, 2015). Its implementation requires the cooperation of multiple actors. Local governments are responsible for the scheme's operations. The National Fund for Family Benefits and the Social Agricultural Mutual Fund process applications, assess eligibility, define the amount of the income support quarterly, and manage the payment of benefits. Finally, the Public Employment Agency provides job counselling and matching services to the scheme's beneficiaries.

4. The impact of the RSA on people's lives

As of June 2015, 2.45 million households were receiving the RSA, out of which 1.6 million did not have economically active members and received the basic allocation only (CNAF, 2015). It is estimated that 68 per cent of the population eligible for the Activity RSA is not registered, notably due to a lack of understanding of the mechanism (Sirugue, 2013).

The RSA provides greater income security and support for people of working age. The scheme also fosters return to work for unemployed people and economic inclusion of the working poor.

58. Innovations to extend coverage

The RSA National Evaluation Committee's final report of 2011 (Comité d'évaluation du RSA, 2011) concluded that the Activity RSA had increased the median income per consumption unit by 18 per cent from 699 Euros (€) to €825 as of December 2009. The scheme also decreased poverty by 0.3 percentage points in 2010, which represent 135,000 people moving out of poverty.

Although the RSA clearly provides incentives to work, the direct impact of the programme on employment is difficult to assess since most beneficiaries receive a number of complementary transfers and other support. Results also significantly differ according to the composition of the household, in particular the number of children.

Regarding potential undesired effects of the RSA, the 2011 evaluation report (Comité d'évaluation du RSA, 2011) shows that concerns about employers using the Activity RSA strategically to decrease wages or impose part-time jobs were not confirmed.

5. What's next?

The RSA is facing three main challenges:
- The efficiency of the RSA is hampered by difficulties in coordinating the actions of participating agencies and government bodies. Local governments that were designated to oversee the implementation of the scheme did not always have the necessary capacities to do so. Additionally, with the global financial crisis and a significant rise in unemployment, the national employment agency is overwhelmed by demand and cannot always provide adapted assistance to RSA beneficiaries.
- The complexity of the scheme has prevented its expansion. Although RSA is well-known, few understand how benefits are calculated, can name its different components, or know the eligibility criteria.
- Finally, the RSA competes with another measure called Employment Bonus (Prime pour l'emploi in French). The

Employment Bonus is a tax credit that has the same objective as the Activity RSA and reaches 6.3 million households.

As a result of these limitations, the French Government has created an Activity Bonus (Prime d'activité) that will replace the Employment Bonus and Activity RSA starting from January 2016 (Government of France, 2015). The Activity Bonus will keep the salient features of the Activity RSA, notably linking the allowance with occupational income. Eligibility criteria will also be simplified.

6. References

CNAF. 2015. RSA conjuncture n°11. Available at: www.caf.fr/sites/default/files/cnaf/Documents/Dser/rsa%20con joncture/Rsa%20Conjoncture%20n%C2%B0%2011_RSA.pdf.

Comité d'évaluation du RSA. 2011. Rapport final. Available at: www.ladocumentationfrancaise.fr/var/storage/rapports-publics/114000721/0000.pdf.

Commission Familles, vulnérabilité, pauvreté. 2015. La nouvelle équation sociale. Available at: www.ladocumentationfrancaise.fr/var/storage/rapports-publics/054000264.pdf.

French Family Allowance Fund. 2015. French Family Allowance Fund website. Available at: www.caf.fr/aides-et-services/s-informer-sur-les-aides/solidarite-et-insertion/le-revenu-de-solidarite-active-rsa.

Government of France. 2008. Law n°2008-1249 of the 1st of December 2008 on the Active Solidarity Income and the reform of social inclusion policies. Available at: www.legifrance.gouv.fr/affichTexte.do?cidTexte=JORFTEXT0000 19860428&dateTexte=&categorieLien=id.

—. 2015. Law n°2015-994 of the 17th August 2015 on social dialogue and employment. Available at: www.legifrance.gouv.fr/affichTexte.do?cidTexte=JORFTEXT0000 31046061&categorieLien=id.

Hirsch, M. 2011. Secu: Objectif monde, le défi universel de la protection sociale (Paris).

Observatoire des inégalités. 2014. Observatoire des inégalités website. Available at: www.inegalites.fr.

Observatoire national de l'action sociale. 2015. La lettre de l'Odas, juin 2015. Available at: http://odas.net/IMG/pdf/lettre_de_l_odas_- _de_penses_de_partementales_d_action_sociale_2015.pdf.

Sirugue, C. 2013. Rapport à M. le Premier ministre - Réforme des dispositifs de soutien aux revenus d'activité modestes. Available at: www.ladocumentationfrancaise.fr/var/storage/rapports- publics/134000431.pdf.

7

India: Mahatma Gandhi National Rural Employment Guarantee Scheme[13]

Enacted on 7 September 2005, the Mahatma Gandhi National Rural Employment Guarantee Act (MGNREGA) in India entitles, by demand, every rural household to a minimum of 100 days of paid work each year at minimum wage. The ensuing public works programme represents an innovative rights-based approach towards supporting income security of rural households while creating productive assets and strengthening local governance.

The first phase of the Mahatma Gandhi National Rural Employment Guarantee Scheme (MGNREGS) was launched in February 2006. Initially covering 200 of the poorest districts, all districts with sizeable rural populations were eventually included by 1 April 2008 (DRD, 2014). MGNREGS is the largest public works programme in the world, providing unskilled manual work to 57.8 million adults from 38.9 million rural households during the fiscal year of 2014-15 (MORD, 2015).

1. Main lessons learned

- Since its inception in 2006, MGNREGS has provided an alternative source of income to workers in rural areas, particularly women and economically backward

---

[13] This chapter was authored by Cheng Boon Ong and Loveleen De of the ILO and reviewed by Valérie Schmitt, Christina Behrendt and Celine Peyron-Bista of the ILO. It was first published in September 2016.

communities, created productive assets and empowered the local Panchayati Raj Institutions (PRIs) through the implementation and monitoring processes.

- A recent ILO study concludes that MGNREGA satisfies many of the provisions under the ILO Social Protection Floor Recommendation, 2012 (No. 202), such as "universality of protection", "entitlement to benefits prescribed by national law", "social inclusion" and "respect for the rights and dignity of people covered by the social security guarantees" (Ehmke, 2015). The legal framework of MGNREGA also reinforces programme sustainability.

- To realize the full potential of an ambitious programme like MGNREGS, policy-makers and implementing agents will need to address several key issues, such as limited public awareness, low administrative and delivery capacities (with large gaps between states), low quality control of assets created and ineffective monitoring and auditing mechanisms (CAG, 2013).

- In states and localities where MGNREGS has been implemented well, many of its social and economic objectives are found to have been achieved (Ehmke, 2015). MGNREGS serves as a South-South learning example for developing countries looking to design and implement public works programmes targeted at poor rural households and deliver the social protection floor.

2. Why was there a need for MGNREGS?

Almost 270 million people live below the poverty line in India, 80.3 per cent of them in rural areas (RBI, 2014). Poverty and unemployment increasingly afflict the growing population of small and marginal farmers and landless agricultural labourers, fuelling mass migration to urban areas (Sharma, 2011). Poverty is most acute among female-headed households and marginalized communities, namely the scheduled castes (SCs) and scheduled tribes (STs).

MGNREGS was introduced in the context of the then-ruling Government's inclusive growth and rights-based policies that recognized social and economic development as entitlements of citizens. MGNREGS aims to:

- provide an alternative source of income during the low agricultural season and poor monsoons;
- empower grassroots governance;
- create durable assets such as roads and irrigation canals that would generate sustainable rural livelihoods and discourage migration to urban areas; and
- encourage conservation of the environment.

3. How does the programme work?

MGNREGA enforces the right of Indian citizens to work and is based on certain articles of the Indian constitution. The programme is demand-based and self-targeting for rural households who are in need of minimum income support. During the fiscal year 2014-15, MGNREGS employed 57.8 million workers, approximately 16.9 per cent of the rural labour force (MORD, 2015; Misra and Suresh, 2014).

MGNREGA is modelled on the principles of transparency and grassroots democracy. It stipulates decentralized administration and governance, in line with which, every state implements its own MGNREGS and funds it jointly with the national Ministry of Rural Development (MORD). Most of the planning, implementation, monitoring and evaluation activities are delegated to the local PRIs.

The uniqueness of MNGREGS lies in its largely bottom-up, multi-agency and multi-level processes for proposing works, registering beneficiaries, financing and sharing costs, measuring output and paying wages (see Figure 14). At the lowest level, the Gram Sabha (village assembly) is designated with recommending appropriate projects. The elected Gram Panchayat (village committee) is responsible for decision-making, planning and implementation (at least 50 per cent of works by law).

Work should be provided within a 5-kilometre radius of the village, otherwise monetary compensation is given for the additional travel and living expenses. If work is not provided within 15 days of a worker's application, state governments are liable to provide an unemployment cash benefit. Contractors and labour-replacing machinery are banned and at most 40 per cent of the total project cost can be used for materials, skilled labour and administrative costs. The rest is safeguarded as wages for beneficiaries performing unskilled manual work.

NREGASoft is a specialized management information system used for management and monitoring of MGNREGS.

Figure 14: Work flow of India's MGNREGS

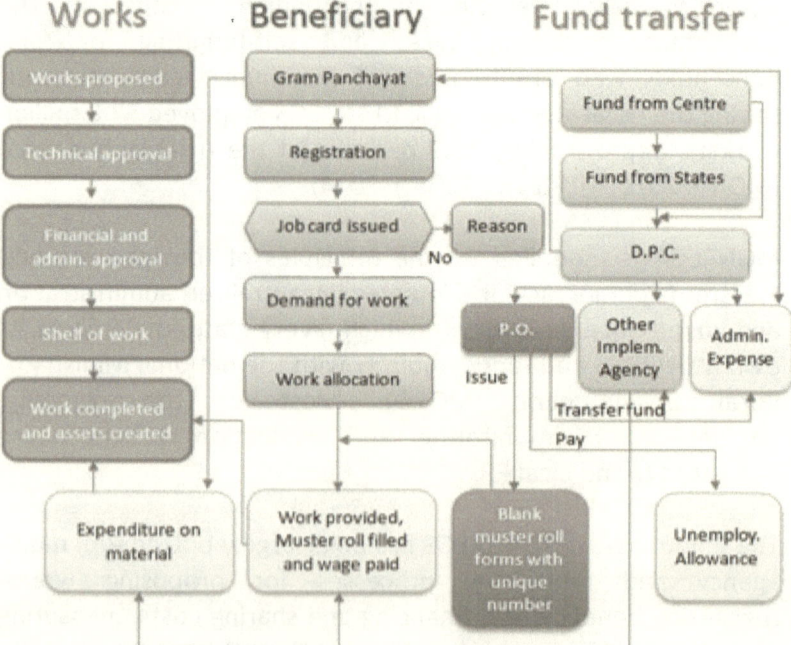

D.P.C.: District Planning Committee. P.O.: Post Office.
Source: MORD 2015, www.nrega.nic.in.

4. How has MGNREGS performed in recent years?

By design, the MGNREGA fulfils many of the provisions under Recommendation No. 202, such as universality of protection, entitlement to benefits prescribed by national law, social inclusion and respect for the rights and dignity of people (Ehmke, 2015). Administrative data from 2014-15 show that MGNREGS has been successful at ensuring the participation of women and the disadvantaged SC and ST communities. More than half (54.5 per cent) of the work provided has benefited women while 39.1 per cent has benefited SC and ST communities. With 98 million new bank/post office accounts opened for MGNREGS work payments, it has encouraged the financial inclusion of the rural poor (MORD, 2015).

However, some rural households, especially the poor, remain excluded from the scheme due to a lack of awareness or inability to perform manual work (Ehmke, 2015). Figure 15 illustrates the estimated MGNREGS coverage rate, i.e. the proportion of rural households that have expressed the desire to work and received work, based on the National Sample Survey 2009/10. Nationally, 56 per cent of households that expressed the desire to work received work. Differences across states are large, varying between 16 and 85 per cent. This being said, almost all households that have officially demanded work were allocated work. This shows that there are several households who are in need of the benefits but do not demand work.

Despite contributing to poverty reduction among rural households, the scheme has faced several setbacks. Some of the problems identified during the public audit carried out by the Comptroller and Auditor General of India (CAG) include shortage of staff, insufficient public awareness of the scheme, lack of effective monitoring and audit mechanisms at the local levels and late wage payments, which reduce the reliability of the scheme as a livelihood coping mechanism (CAG, 2013). Furthermore, the decentralized organization of MGNREGS does not fully address the large inter-state differences in administrative and service delivery capacities (Ehmke, 2015). In particular, states with large populations of rural poor – Bihar, Maharashtra and Uttar Pradesh – have been found to underutilize central Government funds to implement MGNREGS (CAG, 2013).

Figure 15: Coverage rates India's MGNREGS, 2009-10

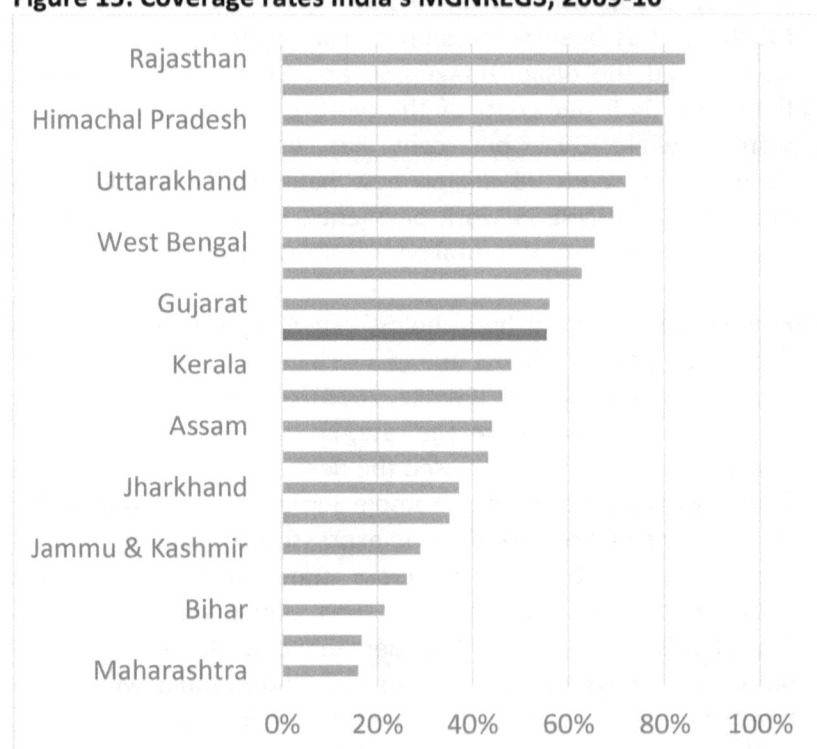

Source: Adapted from Dutta et al., 2012.

5. What's next?

To increase the effectiveness of MGNREGS, the following steps, among others, have been identified (CAG, 2013):
- hire more staff where there are staff shortages;
- utilize Information, Education and Communication funds to increase beneficiary awareness;

- encourage state governments to pay unemployment allowances through co-funding and monitoring; and
- improve administrative records and monitoring, especially at the local level, to evaluate the performance of MGNREGS, ensure compliance and prevent misappropriation of funds.

MGNREGS has since introduced guidelines on compensation for late wage payments, initiated mass media campaigns and provided financial assistance to states for the staffing of social audit units and training of MGNREGS staff (MORD, 2015).

6. References

Comptroller and Auditor General of India (CAG). 2013. Performance audit of Mahatma Gandhi National Rural Employment Scheme (Ministry of Rural Development).

Dutta, P. et al. 2012. Does India's employment guarantee scheme guarantee employment? World Bank Policy Research Working Paper No. 6003.

Ehmke, E. 2015. India's Mahatma Gandhi National Rural Employment Guarantee Scheme, Extension of Social Security (ESS) Paper No. 49 (Geneva, International Labour Organization).

Ministry of Law and Justice. 2005. The National Rural Employment Guarantee Act, The Gazette of India, DL-(N)04/0007/2003-05.

Ministry of Rural Development, Department of Rural Development (DRD). 2015. Mahatma Gandhi National Rural Employment Guarantee Act, 2005: Report to the People, 2 February 2015 (New Delhi).

Ministry of Rural Development (MORD). The Mahatma Gandhi National Rural Employment Guarantee Act 2005. Available at:

http://nrega.nic.in/netnrega/home.aspx [Accessed: 28 May 2015].

Misra, S.; Suresh, A.K. 2014. Estimating employment elasticity of growth for the Indian economy, Reserve Bank of India Working Paper Series.

Reserve Bank of India (RBI). 2014. Handbook of Statistics on Indian Economy 2013-14 (Mumbai).

Sharma, A. 2011. "The Mahatma Gandhi National Rural Employment Guarantee Act – India", in United Nations Development Programme (UNDP) and International Labour Organization (eds.): Successful Social Protection Floor Experiences. Sharing Innovative Experiences (New York), pp. 271–290.

8

Malaysia: Employment injury insurance[14]

The contributory social security system in Malaysia provides income security to employees and their dependents in cases of work-related accidents and occupational disease, as well as non-work-related invalidity and death. The scheme is supplemented by a holistic network of services, including occupational safety and health promotion programmes, healthy lifestyle campaigns and rehabilitation centres that prevent accidents and diseases and facilitate the reintegration of injured workers into the workforce.

The Social Security Organisation of Malaysia (SOCSO) is the main public institution governing the provision and management of the Employment Injury Insurance (EII) and Invalidity Pension (IP) schemes. SOCSO has been running the schemes for more than 40 years and is recognized for its practices in prevention of work-related injuries as well as rehabilitation of injured workers. SOCSO complements the EII and IP schemes by providing support services through its Occupational Safety and Health Promotion programme, Health Screening programme and Return to Work programme in its newly established Rehabilitation Centres.

---

[14] This chapter was authored by Stefan Urban with contributions from Cheng Boon Ong of the ILO and reviewed by Anne Drouin and Valérie Schmitt of the ILO. It was first published in September 2016.

1. Main lessons learned

- Contrary to employers' liability programmes, EII schemes anchored in a strong legal framework protect employers against the financial consequences of catastrophic accidents. Thanks to EII, brands and buyers are no longer held responsible for compensating injured workers in factories.
- Income security provided by EII and IP schemes secures the purchasing power of injured workers and dependents of deceased workers to smooth aggregate demand and consumption.
- The Occupational Safety and Health Promotion programme and healthy lifestyle campaigns reduce the incidence of work-related accidents and diseases and therefore reduce the costs of the EII and IP schemes.
- The Return to Work programme, Rehabilitation Centres and Vocational Rehabilitation help injured and disabled workers to recover and rejoin the workforce faster. This not only supports families and the effective functioning of the labour market, but extends the contribution base of existing schemes.

2. How did the employment injury and invalidity pension schemes develop?

The Employment Injury Insurance Scheme and Invalidity Pension Scheme were created in 1969 and are legislated by the Employees' Social Security Act of 1969.

Employees are eligible to participate in the EII and IP schemes if they are Malaysian citizens, earn no more than 4,000 Malaysian Ringgits (MYR) per month or, when their monthly wages exceed MYR4,000, if they have previously contributed to the schemes or have a mutual agreement with their employer.

Foreigners are not covered by the scheme. As of 2016, coverage is extended to the self-employed, own-account workers, workers of the informal sector, business owners and to the liberal professions.

As of December 2014, SOCSO had 948,219 registered employers and 15.25 million registered employees. Among the latter, 6.2 million were active contributors while 570,625 were recipients of benefits. A total number of 63,331 accident cases were reported in 2014, with a reduction of 0.36 per cent in comparison to the previous year. Of these accidents, 55.73 per cent were industrial accidents, while the remaining were commuting accidents.

3. What benefits are provided?

The EII scheme provides compensation to employees who suffer from accidents and occupational disease arising out of and in the course of employment, including commuting accidents. The IP scheme provides compensations to injured workers and to dependents of deceased workers irrespective of the causes of injuries and deaths.

The contribution rate of the EII scheme is set at 1.25 per cent of insurable earnings and is solely borne by employers, while the contribution rate of the IP scheme is set at 1 per cent of insurable earnings, equally shared by employers and workers.

Benefits under the EII scheme include medical, temporary disablement, permanent disablement, dependents', funeral and education benefits, as well as allowances to attend medical rehabilitation sessions. Benefits provided under the IP scheme include invalidity pensions and grants, survivors' pensions, funeral benefits and rehabilitation benefits.

EII benefits are provided to employees in cases of: (1) industrial accidents while carrying out their duties; (2) accidents while travelling on a route between the employee's home and the place of work, on a work-related journey or on a journey between work and where the employee takes a meal during any authorized recess; (3) accidents during emergencies, occurring in or near the workplace or while assisting in an emergency (rescuing, protecting other people from disaster or any form of danger); and (4) occupational diseases.

Benefits of the EII scheme are classified into short- and long-term benefits. Short-term benefits include medical and rehabilitation benefits, temporary disability benefits and funeral benefits. Long-term benefits refer to permanent disability benefits and dependents' benefits provided in principle in the form of pensions for life, although partly or fully converted into a lump sum under specified conditions. The amount of pension depends on the salary of the insured and, in the case of permanent disability benefits, on the degree of disability, but does not depend on a past service period of the individual.

4. What are the complementary services provided?

The EII and IP schemes provide a variety of complementary services to promote health and safety, to improve peoples' ability to return to work (RTW), to recover from accidents and to develop new skills and capacities in case of job relocation. These services, the RTW programme in particular, are embedded in legislation.

Promoting occupational safety and health

Central to SOCSO is the promotion of awareness for occupational safety and health (OSH) and a healthy lifestyle. In 2014, 248 programmes were carried out by SOCSO across the country, including the Best Practice in Implementing Commuting Safety Management, National Safe Commuting to Work Campaign and Commuting Accident Prevention Seminars.

Encouraging a healthy lifestyle
In 2013, SOCSO introduced its Health Screening Programme, aimed at improving its members' health, in particular concerning non-communicable diseases (NCDs). Free health checks are given to all SOCSO contributors aged 40 years and above who are actively working. Since its inception, the SOCSO Health Screening Programme has been offered to more than 1.9 million contributors. A total of 3,262 private clinics, including laboratories and mammography centres, provide their services to the beneficiaries of the programme nationwide.

The Return to Work programme (RTW)
The RTW programme was introduced by SOCSO in 2007. This physical rehabilitation programme assists employees suffering from disabilities to recover and re-join the workforce.

The programme is implemented through a systematic case management system. The case manager performs a variety of tasks to ensure a consistent and systematic management of the rehabilitation process and to ensure that the injured worker returns to work. These tasks include an initial assessment of the individuals' needs, followed by recommendations regarding workplace modifications or provisions of specialized medical treatments. Modifications at the workplace include adjustments in job scope, tasks, working hours and of workplace. If RTW participants are unable to return to their former employer, they are entitled to receive assistance in job matching and placement, including new skills and vocational training that are required for new occupations. Participants also receive a rehabilitation allowance of MYR20 per day to encourage medical rehabilitation session attendance. Through an RTW monitoring mechanism, qualitative assessments on depression, anxiety, stress and several self-perceived psychosocial outcomes are carried out and help to adjust the rehabilitation process.

In 2014, the programme provided rehabilitation to 2,583 insured members. In total since its start in 2007, 10,643 members have been able to return to work after rehabilitation. Cases are usually processed within one year upon referral. As indicated in Figure 16, out of 2,475 referred cases in 2012, approximately 45 per cent of the insured persons have been re-employed during that year, of which most (79.4 per cent) have returned to the same or similar job with the same employer as before their injury or disability (SOCSO, 2013).

Figure 16: Status of participants in Malaysia, 2012

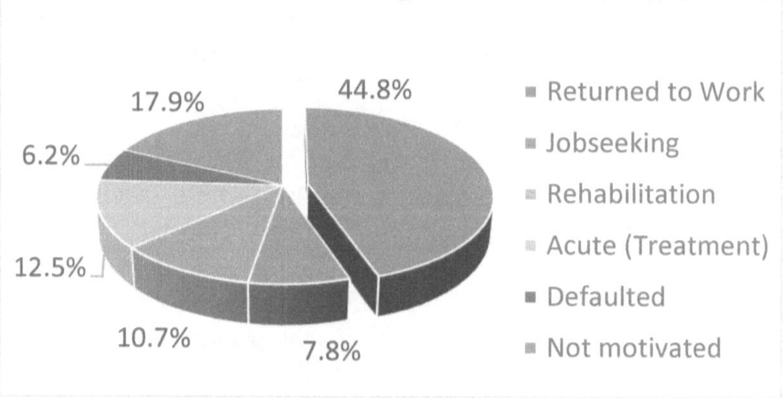

Note: There were 2,475 RTW referred cases in 2012 alone.
Source: Based on data from SOCSO, 2013.

Rehabilitation Centres
The SOCSO Rehabilitation Centres provide rehabilitation services aimed at restoring the insured members' capacities to the needs of work. SOCSO has contracted a number of health professionals and service providers to offer these rehabilitation services, including the development of rehabilitation plans (which is usually done by medical professionals), physical rehabilitation, vocational and occupational rehabilitation, prosthetic/orthotic providers and many others.

SOCSO Education Loan Benefit
SOCSO Education Loan Benefit provides loans or scholarships to dependent children of insured persons. The applicant must be a dependent child of an insured person who dies because of an employment injury or due to an unspecified cause before the

age of 55 years and meets the eligibility requirements of the survivor.

5. What's next?

Malaysia has been successful in building a comprehensive EII and IP system over the past decades by providing a wide range of benefits, complemented by support services that promote health and safety and the reintegration and rehabilitation of insured members.

Health promotion is an ongoing process rather than a one-time event. Consistent communication with insured workers and their families about health and well-being are essential.

A possibility of extending the coverage of the EII scheme to foreign workers should be considered to make the scheme truly comprehensive. Foreign workers are currently covered under the Workmen's Compensation Act and the benefit amounts are much lower than those under the SOCSO scheme. Extending coverage to the self-employed, own-account workers, workers of the informal sector, business owners and to the liberal professions starting in 2016 will most probably raise new challenges.

Some of SOCSO's new Rehabilitation Centres have encountered difficulties with un-adapted infrastructure. The number of days that it takes on average to manage a case needs to be reduced. Additional efforts are also needed to alleviate stigma and other cultural factors that can impede people's participation of the RTW programme, and to extend coverage to non-participating members, including those who are not motivated to participate or have left the programme prematurely.

6. References

Binti R.M.; Merican A.R. 2010. "Employees` Rights under the Malaysian Social Security Organisation", in Journal of Politics and Law, Vol. 3, No. 1, pp. 24-44.

Cheong, E.P.H. 2014. "Developing the Social Security Organisation (SOCSO) of Malaysia's RTW case management system", in International Journal of Disability Management, Vol. 9.

ILO. 2014. World Social Protection Report 2014/2015 (Geneva).

Social Security Organization (SOCSO). 2015. Annual Report 2014 (Kuala Lumpur).

—. 2015. A Guide for Return to Work Coordinators (Kuala Lumpur).

Vadivel, G. 2015. Moving from Payer to Player in Occupation Injuries and Accidents - The Case of Malaysia, paper presented at the 1st Namibian Social Protection Conference, Windhoek, 8 July.

9

Philippines: Integrated Livelihood and Emergency Employment Programme [15]

The Philippine Department of Labor and Employment's (DOLE) Integrated Livelihood and Emergency Employment Programme (DILEEP) provides employment and entrepreneurship opportunities to displaced, disadvantaged, and unemployed workers.

A major component of the Philippine social protection system, DILEEP links disaster and climate risk management with social security and active labour market policies. It provides short-term wage employment and facilitates entrepreneurship for people affected by natural calamities and economic shocks, as well as enrols beneficiaries in social insurance.

DILEEP responds to the President's Social Contract with the Filipino People 2011, which calls for veering away "from anti-poverty government programmes (...), to well-considered programmes that build capacity and create opportunities among the poor and the marginalized". DILEEP was implemented in the wake of Typhoon Haiyan and benefitted 79,655 affected workers.

---

[15] This chapter was authored by Loveleen De of the ILO and reviewed by Isabel Ortiz, Valérie Schmitt, Celine Peyron-Bista and Clara van Panhuys of the ILO. It was first published in April 2015.

1. Main lessons learned

- DILEEP shows that social protection systems combined with employment programmes can help build the resilience of populations at risk of natural disasters.
- DILEEP promotes a comprehensive approach to decent work for workers in the informal sector. Beneficiaries are paid at the prevailing regional minimum wage, registered with social security and health insurance, and trained in workplace safety.
- DILEEP highlights that pre-existing administrative capacity of social protection and employment programmes can improve the readiness and ability of countries to set up emergency measures and reconstruction programmes in the event of natural disasters.
- DILEEP confirms that cooperation and coordination between government departments and local administrations is necessary to maximize outreach and effectiveness. This is an on-going effort in the Philippines which, as a nation, has adequate coordination at the policy level, but low coordination at the implementation level.

2. Vulnerability to disasters and high unemployment

The Philippines is one of the most vulnerable countries to natural disasters in the world; on average, 20 typhoons strike the country every year, affecting millions of people and their livelihoods. Despite strong GDP growth (7.2 per cent in 2013), it has high unemployment and underemployment, which were recorded at 6.8 per cent and 18.4 per cent, respectively, in 2014. The benefits of growth have not been distributed evenly and Filipino society is highly inequitable, with 25.8 per cent of the population considered poor and 41.6 per cent vulnerably employed as of July 2014 (PSA, 2014).

In light of the high vulnerability to socio-economic risks and natural disasters, the Philippine Government prioritizes the provision of social protection and the reduction of poverty and inequality. The Philippine Development Plan 2011-2016 includes the provision of disaster sensitive social protection, employment and income support to affected people, which is provided through DILEEP, as depicted in Figure 17.

Figure 17: Linkages of Philippines' DILEEP with national strategic plans

Source: DOLE and TWGC, 2013.

The DOLE Integrated Livelihood and Emergency Employment Programme was initiated in 2009 in response to the global economic crisis. It aims to restore livelihoods and provide immediate social protection to vulnerable, unemployed, underemployed, and displaced workers, and survivors of calamities. This is done by providing short-term employment in infrastructure and non-infrastructure projects involving the clearance of debris, rebuilding of roads and shelters, reforestation, coastal resource management, and other work. DILEEP also assists self-employed people by facilitating their access to credit and training (ILO, 2014).

3. Decent employment and livelihood rebuilding

Typhoon Haiyan, one of the strongest typhoons to have ever made landfall, struck the central Philippines in November 2013, wiping out the lives of over 7,000 people and affecting the livelihoods of 5.9 million workers, 2.6 million of whom were already vulnerably employed and living at or near the poverty line (ILO, 2013). Typhoon Hagupit made landfall in the Philippines in December 2014, causing one million evacuations and destroying significant infrastructure.

In the aftermath of the typhoons, DILEEP was swiftly put into place by the Department of Labor and Employment (DOLE) in cooperation with the ILO, the Department of Social Welfare and Development (DSWD), and other government agencies. The work performed by typhoon victims included cleaning and repairing public infrastructure and buildings, unclogging canals, and clearing and sorting debris. The goal was to enable people to rebuild their communities while simultaneously being granted social protection and temporary income support.

The ILO provides technical and financial assistance to DOLE and works with the programme to ensure that beneficiaries of DILEEP are not only paid at the prevailing regional minimum wage, but also given access to health insurance through the national PhilHealth programme, accident insurance through the Government Service Insurance System (GSIS), orientation on occupational safety and health (OSH), and access to Training for Work Scholarships. PhilHealth and GSIS contributions are paid by the Government (ILO, 2014). In this way, DILEEP follows a rights-based approach to decent working conditions while supporting beneficiaries in their search for better livelihood opportunities.

"Emergency employment was an important part of the Government's response. The standards ensure that worker-beneficiaries receive 100 per cent of the regional minimum wage, orientations on basic OSH, personal protective equipment and social insurance. This followed our shared conviction that not just any work would do; we need to maximize every effort to help our countrymen."

- Benigno S. Aquino III, President of the Philippines

DILEEP is an umbrella programme that consists of several interventions targeted at specific vulnerable groups, including displaced workers, fishermen, women workers, and persons with disabilities. The major interventions include: Tulong Pangkabuhayan sa Ating Disadvantaged Workers, which provides wage employment for 10 to 30 days to every beneficiary and social protection, Integrated Services for Livelihood Advancement which gives working capital to seaweed farmers and fishermen, Kabuhayan for managing employment under non-infrastructure projects, and Entrepreneurship Development Assistance and others (ILO, 2014).

DOLE is the main department in charge of DILEEP. Due to the geographical nature of the country, the population is widely dispersed across its 7,000 islands, making it necessary for DOLE to coordinate with its regional offices and accredited co-partners in implementing social protection programmes. Accredited co-partners include local government units, government and non-government organizations, and civil society organizations that have undergone a verification process (ILO, 2014).

DILEEP assisted 79,655 people who were affected by Typhoon Haiyan (DOLE, 2014). Data on the number of projects and beneficiaries is recorded by DOLE and consolidated in the Community-based Employment Programme (CBEP) Online Monitoring and Reporting System, which is a common monitoring system for all government-run projects.

DILEEP is backed by Executive and Department Orders. Funds are sourced from the government budget through the Adjustment Measures Program, and from external donors (ILO, 2014).

4. Measurable impact on beneficiaries' lives

According to DOLE Secretary Rosalinda Dimapilis-Baldoz, DILEEP has had a considerable impact as 90 per cent of beneficiaries have seen increased incomes, while 45 per cent were able to generate employment out of their livelihood projects. Additionally, 417,009 informal sector workers who were supported by DILEEP between 2010 and 2014 are now self-employed and earning from their ventures (DOLE, 2014).

DILEEP helps rehabilitate communities and encourages and trains people to build sustainable community-based enterprises through the efficient use of locally available resources and raw materials. It also develops awareness of social security by enrolling the beneficiaries in PhilHealth and GSIS, while also introducing them to OSH.

5. Challenges and next steps

In the Philippines, there are many interventions targeting disaster victims with limited coordination between them. For instance, there is overlap in targeting of beneficiaries between DILEEP and DSWD's cash-for-work intervention. DSWD also operates other social assistance interventions, including conditional cash transfers, community-driven development, and entrepreneurial support. The implementation of these schemes needs to be harmonized with those run by DOLE.

Over the next two years, DOLE will improve the beneficiary identification system. This will be done through a comprehensive profiling of informal sector workers. The implementation is also expected to become more decentralized with greater expansion at the grassroots.

6. References

Department of Labor and Employment (DOLE). 2014. "90 per cent of livelihood beneficiaries report increased incomes; 45 per cent created more community employment", in DOLE News, 1 Sep. Available at: www.dole.gov.ph.

—. 2015. Official website. Available at: www.dole.gov.ph [11 Mar. 2015].

—; Technical Working Group Committee (TWGC). 2013. Community-Based Employment Program reference manual Vol. 1 (Manila). Available at: www.dole.gov.ph/cbep [12 Mar. 2015].

Department of Social Welfare and Development (DSWD). 2015. Official website. Available at: www.dswd.gov.ph [11 Mar. 2015].

Employees' Compensation Commission (ECC). 2012. The Social Protection Operational Framework and Strategy in the Philippines, presented at the Social Protection Floor Consultation, Manila, 22 Nov.

Government of the Philippines. 2013. Draft Social Protection Plan, presented at the Consultation Workshop on Finalization of the Social Protection Plan, Manila, 11-12 Sep.

International Labour Organization (ILO). 2013. "ILO supports DOLE's emergency employment programmes", in ILO News, 9 Dec. Available at: www.ilo.org/manila [11 Mar. 2015].

—. 2014. Philippines: Assessment based national dialogue on social protection, employment promotion and disaster management. Available at: www.social-protection.org [11 Mar. 2015].

84. Innovations to extend coverage

Official Gazette of the Republic of the Philippines. 2009. "Executive Order No. 783, s. 2009", 13 Feb. Available at: www.gov.ph [Accessed: 11 March 2015].

Philippine Statistics Authority (PSA). 2014. Labour Force Survey: Annual labor and employment status 2014 (Manila). Available at: www.psa.gov.ph [17 Apr. 2015].

10

Romania: Builders' Social Fund[16]

A bipartite sectoral approach for construction workers: Since 1998, Romania's Builders' Social Fund, or Casa Socială a Constructorilor (CSC), has provided income protection for workers in the construction sector during the interruption of work in winter.[17] The CSC is a non-profit organization based on a sectoral social agreement. It operates on a bipartite basis. It is governed by a general assembly which is composed of representatives of social partners.

Following the implementation of the CSC, social partners made a sectoral social agreement to extend its scope. Today the CSC provides a wider range of services for the construction sector in Romania.

1. Main lessons learned

- By providing income support and job security against the risk of seasonal unemployment, the CSC improves working conditions in the construction sector in Romania.
- The benefits and services of the CSC contribute to prevent informal employment in the construction sector.

---

[16] This chapter was authored by Kenichi Hirose of the ILO with the assistance of Daria Copil and Lara Polus who are former interns of the ILO and reviewed by Isabel Ortiz, Valérie Schmitt and Loveleen De of the ILO. It was first published in February 2016.
[17] Law No. 215 of 1997 on the Builders' Social Fund, published in the Official Gazette No. 372 on 22 December 1997.

- The CSC has expanded its services to provide vocational training, cover selected medical and pharmaceutical costs and conduct safety inspections in selected construction sites.
- The CSC is based on a joint initiative of social partners at the sectoral level. The involvement of workers' and employers' representatives ensures ownership and dialogue in the policy making process.
- The financial contribution of the construction sector not only adds a unique characteristic to this sector-based bilateral scheme, but also provides a crucial source of financing for the CSC.
- The CSC has limitations inherent to a sector-based welfare organization; the scheme is exposed to risks due to changes in the economy and the construction sector. These can be overcome by having larger national public schemes.

2. What is the coverage of CSC?

CSC covers workers employed in construction companies and manufacturers of building materials in Romania. Its coverage is voluntary in two ways: (i) an employer in the construction sector can decide to become a member of the CSC; and (ii) an employee of a member company can decide whether or not to join the CSC.[18]

Table 2 presents data on CSC coverage for 2010-14. In 2013, CSC covered 70,800 workers or 13.8 per cent of employees in the construction sector. However, due to the economic downturn which has resulted in a recent contraction of the construction sector in Romania, the CSC lost 28 per cent of its membership in 2014, leaving 50,725 members representing 10.7 per cent of the

---

[18] The CSC is considering the introduction of a voluntary membership option for all employees in construction companies and building material manufacturers irrespective of their employers' CSC membership status.

employees in the sector. It is also reported that the CSC lost 16 per cent of its member companies in 2013.

Table 2: Coverage of the CSC in Romania, 2010-14

	2010	2011	2012	2013	2014
Member companies	356	390	359		
Employees covered	72,025	67,238	68,420	70,800	50,725
Employees covered (% of employees in construction)	14.0	13.2	13.1	13.8	10.7
Employed population in construction	701,600	677,100	674,100	673,400	633,900
Of which: Employees in construction	516,100	508,600	521,300	513,600	473,300

3. What benefits are provided by CSC?

The core activity of the CSC is the provision of a cash benefit called a "cold weather allowance" to cover employees during the interruption of work in winter months (from November to March). The benefits are paid directly to employees based on a payment request from member companies and endorsed by a trade union or employees' representative.

The cash benefit is 75 per cent of the individual employee's average base salary over the last three months and paid in proportion to the interruption of work for a maximum duration of 90 days. The level and duration of the benefit do not depend on the contributions made by individual employees. Throughout the period in which the worker receives the cash benefit, the beneficiary retains their employment status, including seniority, leave, and social insurance coverage.

Table 3 presents the number of beneficiaries and expenditures for the cold weather allowance during 2010-14. In 2014, a total of 21,178 workers received cash benefits, representing 41.8 per cent of the covered employees in the same period. Each beneficiary in 2014 received an average of 1,231 Romanian Lei (RON) (277 Euros - €) for 15 days during the winter months.

Table 3: CSC's cold weather allowance in Romania, 2010-14

	2010	2011	2012	2013	2014
No. of beneficiaries	29,101	31,301	39,010	30,312	21,178
No. of beneficiaries (% of covered workers)	40.4	46.6	57.0	42.8	41.8
Average annual benefit (RON)	986	976	1,092	1,261	1,231
Minimum wage as of 1 Jan (RON)	600	670	700	700	850
Cash benefit expenditure (thousand RON)	28,690	30,540	42,580	38,230	26,060
Average No. of days for which benefits were paid	-	13.9	14.9	15.9	15.0

In contrast, under the current Law on Unemployment Insurance System and Employment Stimulation, the unemployment benefit is payable to involuntarily unemployed persons who have contributed for at least 12 months in the last 24 months before their registration at an employment office.[19] The monthly amount of the unemployment benefit is 75 per cent of the social

---

[19] Law No. 76 of 2002 on the Unemployment Insurance System and Employment Stimulation, published in the Official Gazette No. 103 on 6 February 2002.

reference indicator,[20] plus a salary-related increment ranging from 3 to 10 per cent if the contribution period is three years or longer.[21]

The maximum duration of the unemployment benefit depends on the contribution period: six months if the contribution period is one to five years; nine months if the contribution period is five to ten years; and 12 months if the contribution period is ten years or more. In terms of the average figures in 2014, there were 475,790 registered unemployed workers in Romania and 142,474 unemployment beneficiaries, comprising 30 per cent of the registered unemployed. The average monthly benefit was RON424 (€95) for the unemployed who have made contributions and RON226 (€51) for new graduates.

4. How is CSC financed?

CSC's main source of income comes from contributions paid by the employers and employees of the member companies, and contributions from the construction sector as a whole. The breakdown is as follows:

- Employee contributions equal 1 per cent of the gross base salary.
- Employer contributions equal to 1.5 per cent of the turnover of construction projects.[22]
- Construction sector contributions equal 0.5 per cent of the estimated value of all construction work in Romania, irrespective of CSC membership.

---

[20] The social reference indicator is the base amount of social assistance benefits. In 2015, the social reference indicator was RON500, which is slightly over half the minimum wage.

[21] For new entrants to the labour market, the unemployment benefit at 50 per cent of the social reference indicator is payable for up to six months.

[22] In practice, employers pay their contributions in proportion to the number of their employees covered by the CSC based on the estimated amount of annual turnover.

Table 4: Fund operations of the CSC in Romania, 2010-14 (thousands of RON)

	2010	2011	2012	2013	2014
Total income	**56,020**	**56,180**	**57,190**	**48,940**	**45,540**
Employee contributions (1%)	3,680	3,877	4,079	3,135	2,898
Employer contributions (1.5%)	14,570	14,371	15,969	14,940	8,000
Construction sector contributions (0.5%)	25,460	27,730	25,990	20,790	25,660
Investment income	12,300	10,190	11,150	10,070	8,990
Total expenditures (est.)	**33,650**	**35,370**	**47,810**	**43,000**	**33,160**
Cash benefit	28,690	30,540	42,580	38,230	26,060
Other (est.)	4,960	4,830	5,230	4,770	7,100
Reserve fund	**168,810**	**189,620**	**199,000**	**204,940**	**217,320**
Reserve fund / Benefit exp.	5.0	5.4	4.2	4.8	6.6

In addition, the CSC retains a reserve fund. Income earned from reserve fund investments also adds to the total income of the CSC. The Law also stipulates that the administrative costs should not exceed 10 per cent of the total income of the CSC.

Table 4 presents fund operations of the CSC during 2010-14. The following observations are made:

- Throughout this period, total income of the CSC exceeded its total expenditures with relatively large surpluses. On average, almost half of the CSC's income comes from contributions from the construction sector, more than a quarter comes from employer contributions, and about 20 per cent of total income comes from investment income. Employee contributions account for only 6 to 7 per cent of total income.

- The surpluses in the recent past are largely due to the contributions from the construction sector. Without the sectoral contributions or investment income, the bipartite contributions from employers and employees would cover only 40 to 60 per cent of benefit expenditures.

- There are no data on how many contributions are paid per covered worker per year. Assuming that all covered workers contribute at the minimum wage, it is estimated that the average contribution period was at most 8.5 months per year for 2010-12. In 2013 and 2014, under the same assumption, the average contribution period decreased to at most 6.5 months per year.

- Due to past surpluses, the CSC has accumulated a substantial level of reserve funds. At the end of 2014, the reserve fund totalled RON217.3 million, which equals 6.6 times total annual expenditures. The assets of the CSC were composed of bank deposits (58.7 per cent), government securities and bonds (32.4 per cent), and corporate bonds and Credit Linked Notes (8.9 per cent).

- Benefit expenditures peaked in 2012 and then gradually declined mainly due to the decrease in the number of beneficiaries. Other expenditures, which include administrative costs, had been steady at 9 per cent of total income until 2013. However, these expenditures increased sharply to 15.6 per cent of total income in 2014.

5. How have CSC's services for the construction sector been further expanded?

Since the implementation of the cold weather allowance, the scope of CSC services has gradually expanded to cover various support services aimed to foster the building industry. Since 2001, the CSC started issuing bank guarantee letters to member companies—those who have made contributions—to participate in bidding for new construction projects. The CSC facilitates preferable purchase or exchange of goods and services, including building materials and equipment, between CSC member companies. Furthermore, based on the sectoral social agreement in the construction sector, the following non-profit organizations were subsequently established.

- The **Vocational Training House of Builders** (*Casa de Meserii a Constructorilor* (CMC)), established in 2004, organizes vocational training, issues skill certifications, develops occupational standards.[23]
- The **Occupational Safety and Health House of Builders** (*Casa de Siguranţă în Mediul de Muncă a Constructorilor*), established in 2007, provides consultations and trainings on occupational safety and health and conducts safety inspections in line with the agreement with the State Labour Inspectorates.
- The **Paritarian Committee for Multinational Companies** (*Comitetul Paritar pentru Trusturi Transnaţionale*), established in 2007, provides facilitations between multinational and domestic companies, particularly in the areas of subcontracting and social dialogue.
- The **Paritarian Committee for Migrant and Posted Workers** (*Comitetul Paritar pentru Muncitori Migranţi*),

---

[23] The Sectoral Committee in Construction (*Comitet Sectorial în Construcţii*) was initially established within CMC and was previously called the Sectoral Committee for Vocational Training in Construction. It was reorganized as an independent non-government organization of public utility in 2011, when Law No. 268 of 2009 came into force.

established in 2007, implements the regulation on foreign worker quotas and provides assistance to potential migrant workers.

- The **House of Vacation of Builders** (*Casa de Concedii a Constructorilor*), established in 2007, provides services covering the payment of annual and medical leave and oversees a network of clinics and pharmacies across the country.

The consortium of these non-profit organizations, which together provide comprehensive services for the construction sector, is called the **Self-regulatory Sectoral System in Construction** (*Sistemul de Autoreglementări Sectoriale în Construcții* (SASeC)).

Source: CSC.

6. What are CSC's good practices?

The main advantages of the CSC are summarized here. First, workers have an obvious advantage in securing their income and employment status, including social insurance coverage during the seasonal disruption of construction work. The level of the cold weather allowance is higher than the unemployment benefit, while the qualifying period is shorter.

Second, the CSC benefits provide an incentive for workers (especially skilled workers) to stay in the domestic labour market, thereby preventing the emigration of skilled workers from Romania.

Third, CSC provides member companies with support services, such as bank guarantee letters, preferable access to the commodity market, vocational training, occupational safety and health services, and other business assistance.

Fourth, the CSC contributes to better industrial relations and improved social dialogue. The bipartite structure underpinning the governance of the fund administration ensures ownership and social dialogue in the policy-making process. It also enables social partners to represent their common interest vis-à-vis the Government and other national and international actors.

Fifth, by requiring covered workers to have employment contracts and be registered at local labour inspectorates, the CSC creates an incentive for informally employed workers to move into formal employment. It should be noted that about one third of the workers in the construction sector in Romania are employed informally.

7. What are the challenges and limitations of CSC?

Despite the success of the programme, the CSC still has remaining challenges and limitations.

First, the CSC must further enhance the enrolment of companies and workers, particularly small and medium-sized firms. At the same time, the CSC should take steps to improve compliance and contribution collection with respect to member companies and covered employees. The issue of coverage extension is especially pertinent in view of the contributions collected from the whole construction sector.

Second, yearly surpluses and the cumulative reserve fund can be used to enhance the income security provided by CSC benefits. Subject to a more in-depth assessment, one could develop possible options, including improving the replacement rate of the cold weather allowance, extending the benefit duration, and paying benefits in cases of income stoppage due to other adverse weather conditions (e.g. floods, heat waves, among others).

Third, the CSC has limitations inherent to a sector-based bilateral model. Coverage of a single sector exposes the scheme to risks due to changes in the economy and the industry's employment structure in the domestic labour market, as observed by the recent decline in membership.[24]

Fourth, the CSC takes significant advantage of contributions from the construction sector. Such an advantage may not exist in other sectors. If the replication of a CSC-type scheme in other sectors is to be considered, then benefits have to be designed by taking into account the contributory capacity of employers and workers, as well as the availability of any complementary sources of income.

8. References

Casa Socială a Constructorilor. 2015. Raport Annual 2014 [Annual Report 2014] (Bucharest). Available at: www.casoc.ro/.

Cristescu, D. (ed.). 2015. Sistemul de Autoreglementări Sectoriale în Construcţii (SASeC) XV [Self-regulatory Sectoral System in Construction XV] (Bucharest). Available at: www.sasec.ro.

---

[24] It should be noted that the CSC has been providing support to Moldovan social partners to establish a similar system in the Republic of Moldova.

Law No. 215 of 1997 on the Builders' Social Fund. Available at: www.casoc.ro/index.php/cadrul-legal/5-casoc/cadru-legal/17-legea-215.

Law No. 76 of 2002 on the Unemployment Insurance System and Employment Stimulation. Available at: www.mmuncii.ro/pub/imagemanager/images/file/Legislatie/LEGI/L76-2002_act.pdf.

Institutul Național de Statistică. 2015. Buletin Statistic Lunar, 2/2015 [Monthly Statistical Bulletin 2/2015] (Bucharest). Available at: www.insse.ro/.

Casa de Meserii a Constructorilor [The Vocational Training House of Builders] website: www.cmc.org.ro.

11

Sahel: Social protection in the face of climate change[25] [26]

The effects of climate change are increasingly apparent in many Sahel countries. Relief efforts during weather-related food crises and in response to everyday deprivation have been largely led by outside actors. However, many Sahel countries have now adopted national strategies for social protection expansion, which provides a new opportunity to enshrine at least basic guarantees of a social protection floor in law and address climate-related risks.

Recurrent food crises have become a regular feature of life in the Sahel. Many Sahel countries have developed national strategies for social protection. Countries can design and implement social protection systems with measures for relief in anticipation of or following climate-related shocks. International actors must be ready to incorporate climate considerations into social protection technical assistance.

1. Main lessons learned

- Decades of drought, increasing temperatures and erratic rainfall brought on by climate change have made recurrent food crises a regular feature of life in the Sahel. Extreme rainfall events have become more

---

[25] This chapter was authored by James Canonge with contributions from Loveleen De of the ILO and reviewed by Valérie Schmitt of the ILO. It was first published in September 2016.
[26] Delineations of the "Sahel region" vary. Statistics provided in this brief cover the countries of Burkina Faso, Cameroon, Chad, Gambia, Mali, Mauritania, Niger, Nigeria and Senegal.

frequent over the last decade, with instances of flash flooding and soil erosion increasing.

- International actors play a large role in providing protection in many Sahel countries. Increasingly, however, countries are developing national social protection strategies that would provide protections for a range of risks, including those related to climate change.
- With the consideration of several climate factors when designing and implementing social protection systems, including social protection floors, Sahel countries can provide essential protections for all, while also addressing specific climate-related risks.
- Following climate discussions in Paris, the international community is now tasked with integrating climate factors into efforts to extend essential and sustainable social protection coverage in the Sahel and elsewhere.

2. The climate of the Sahel region is becoming more volatile as a result of climate change

The Sahel region in Africa sits below the arid Sahara desert but above the tropical savannahs and lush rainforests that cover much of the continent. The region, already suffering from protracted rainfall deficits monitored since the 1960s, is proving itself increasingly susceptible to the effects of climate change.

In recent years, the region has suffered long-running food crises and dislocation triggered by spikes in the severity of a drought spanning more than three decades. During that time, food crises have claimed the lives of some 100,000 people and left 750,000 across Mali, Niger and Mauritania dependent upon food assistance.

While the protracted drought yielded consistent rainfall deficits for years, recently a different trend has emerged. Weather conditions in the region are characterized by extreme variations in annual rainfall from one year to the next. Extreme rainfall events have become more frequent during the last decade, with flash flooding and soil erosion occurring more frequently during the rainy period. In 2013, severe flooding was reported in many countries across the Sahel, affecting more than 300,000 residents, damaging houses, infrastructure and crops. This increased volatility, coupled with consistently higher average annual temperatures, is often attributed to the increased concentration of greenhouse gases in the atmosphere.

Following decades of drought, rainfall has become increasingly unpredictable in the Sahel.

Figure 18: Mean annual precipitation in the Sahel region, as per cent of 1950-2004 annual average.

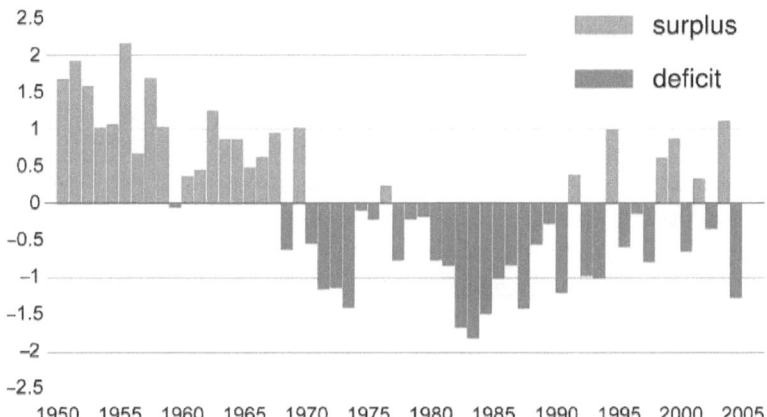

Source: Joint Institute for the Study of the Atmosphere and Ocean (JISAO).

These changes pose considerable challenges to residents who rely on fertile, irrigable land on which to grow crops and graze livestock for their livelihoods. Many of these residents may be forced to seek suitable land elsewhere. Already, it has been observed that traditional nomadic patterns of migration are giving way to more permanent southward movements. If the current trends of unpredictable and extreme rains and temperatures continue, they could lead to a large-scale displacement of people across the region, potentially towards other regions and continents.

While increased unpredictability of weather patterns makes planning more difficult for individual households, it presents new opportunities for governments and their partners to integrate new risk management and coping mechanisms into social protection systems. For the Sahel region in particular, building social protection floors that are resilient against climate shocks and responsive to slow onset events is increasingly being prioritized as economies and societies seek to adapt to the inevitable effects of climate change.

3. Many Sahel countries have only minimal safety net provisions

Some 23.5 million people across the Sahel region are currently food insecure, with roughly 4.5 million children malnourished. The region suffers from chronic poverty, low levels of development and, in recent years, increased instances of armed conflict, the effects of which are only compounded by the looming consequences of a more volatile climate.

Much of the concerted response by Sahel countries to food insecurity in the region has been to address obstacles to food production and sale. The Food Crisis Prevention Network (RPCA), created in 1984, brings together countries in the region with humanitarian and development agencies to share information about agricultural conditions and coordinate food assistance and subsidy planning without distorting local markets or production. Another joint initiative is the creation of a regional agricultural policy among members of the Economic Community of West African States (ECOWAS) that would include the establishment of a Regional Food Security Reserve as a resource in case of a major food crisis while also supporting national and sub-national food storage capacities. Specifically to deal with the impending effects of climate change, a common risk pooling mechanism for African countries, the African Risk Capacity agency, was established under the African Union through which participating governments, including from several Sahel countries, purchase an insurance policy and receive an automatic disbursement to carry out relief activities that would help affected households in the event of extreme rainfall or drought.

Food insecurity has varied widely across the Sahel.

Figure 19: Proportion of undernourished in total population, 2014-16, by country in the Sahel region.

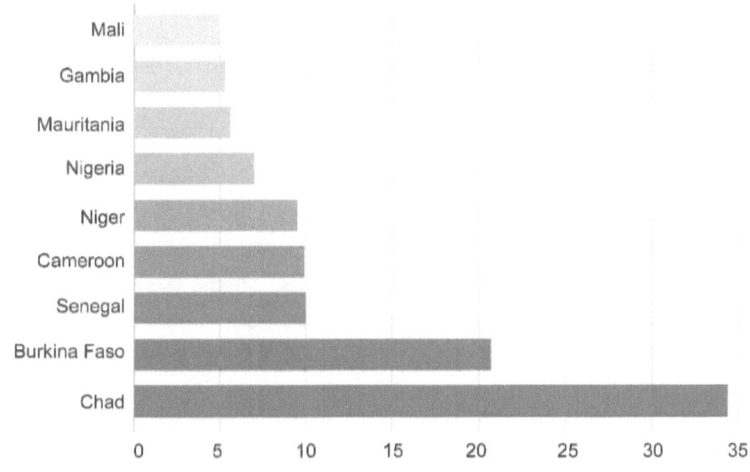

Source: FAO Hunger Map 2015.

Humanitarian and development actors continue to play a large role in social protection provision in countries of the Sahel. Many aim at providing food assistance and health-care services to fight malnutrition, while others support cash-for-work and food-for-work programmes whose beneficiaries perform activities to increase yields and make crops less vulnerable to adverse weather. Since the programmes rely upon external financing and administrative capacities, these protections—in particular those that provide vital cash support—are vulnerable to vacillations in donor funding and priorities. It is precisely for this reason that development actors are now seeking to assist these countries to develop nationally-owned social protection systems. To this end, with support from the European

Commission, several non-governmental organizations have committed to harmonizing targeting approaches and other parameters in their programmes in Mali. The goal is to eventually create a more coherent set of social protection interventions, which could eventually be taken up by the Government and made part of a national social protection system in the country.

Comprehensive social protection systems or social protection floors have yet to take root in most Sahel countries. However, many have developed ambitious national social protection strategies, often with specific references to climate-related risks (e.g. Burkina Faso, Mali, Mauritania and Niger, among others). This often represents a first step in the development of a nationally defined social protection floor. However, implementation remains a challenge due to fiscal and administrative capacity constraints. As development partners formulate technical assistance to support these countries in the rollout of social protection systems to provide at least floor-level provisions, exposure to risks associated with climate change should be considered.

ILO Guidelines for a "just transition"

In October 2015, a tripartite meeting of experts adopted a series of guidelines to ensure a just—or socially and economically equitable—transition towards greener economies and societies. Among the key policy areas covered in the guidelines is social protection. In particular, they suggest, "promot[ing] innovative social protection mechanisms that contribute to offsetting the impacts of climate change and the challenges of the transition on livelihoods, incomes and jobs."

These guidelines were adopted by the ILO's Governing Body in November 2015. The case of the Sahel region illustrates how the ILO guidelines can be applied and social protection policies used to ensure a "just transition."

4. The concept of "climate-ready" social protection is particularly relevant for Sahel countries

In a region like the Sahel, there is a dull roar of deprivation that continues between shocks. This deprivation requires protection measures to realize the universal right to social security. Already, some efforts are underway to establish basic social protection guarantees. However, given this region's particular and increasing vulnerability to the effects of climate change, social protection systems should build in climate and other shock-resilience or response mechanisms to ensure that they continue to provide meaningful and timely protection during and after crises.

To this end, flexible and anticipatory social protection systems can be designed to make regular cash transfer programmes more resilient and efficient following shocks. This makes particular sense in the design of climate-resilient social protection systems where the bulk of the effects manifest themselves as slow onset events, such as persistent environmental degradation, including repetitive floods and droughts, as in the case of the Sahel. Investing in the design of flexible national social protection systems in regions like the Sahel is useful given the inevitability of relatively frequent small- to medium-scale shocks, which are potentially on the rise as a result of global climate change.

Beyond the fundamental institutions and coordination efforts necessary to develop comprehensive systems that provide essential protections, several additional factors can affect the ability of social protection systems to anticipate and respond quickly to climate-related risks relevant to Sahel residents.

National strategies for social protection in Sahel countries

National strategies for social protection that aim to extend coverage for at least essential social protection Sahel countries also make references to the need to address the increased risks faced by many from climate change.

Niger

"Niger commits to a vision of … a social protection policy … to face environmental and climate-related risks."

Burkina Faso

"Social protection aims to … reduce the vulnerability of the population facing climate and environmental risks …"

Mauritania

"… to strengthen the mechanisms to mitigate the effects of climate change on food and nutritional security of vulnerable communities."

Note: Adapted from the original French.

CLIMATE FACTOR 1:

Climate vulnerabilities used in the identification and selection of social protection beneficiaries

Climate vulnerabilities can be incorporated into: identification procedures through risk and vulnerability assessments conducted at different levels of government; selection criteria through needs assessments for social support eligibility; and targeting methods to reach households most vulnerable to climate change-related risks through using area-level and household-level data on climate exposure. These can include geographic or topographic indicators (administrative designations, certain geographical characteristics, such as rugged terrain or proximity to water, or areas prone to extreme weather, such as chronic flooding or drought), or hardship indicators (areas experiencing chronic food insecurity, where damage from a previous hardship has been registered and where previous aid has been delivered). Some of these modalities are already used in other parts of the world. In Bangladesh, for example, poor communities living near rivers vulnerable to flooding are eligible for cash support as part of the Char Livelihoods Project. In Ethiopia, as part of the Productive Safety Net Program (PSNP), residents in areas designated as chronically food insecure are specifically targeted for inclusion as a part of the programme's selection criteria. In Mexico, residents in areas with low average rainfall and rugged terrain are targeted for inclusion in a public works programme, the Programa de Empleo Temporal (PET), to build and upgrade local roads.

CLIMATE FACTOR 2
Emergency protocols to expand eligibility and verification requirements and scale up payments

For existing social protection programmes, particularly those with large beneficiary bases, contingency planning can lead to the development of emergency protocols that, when activated by authorities, can rapidly scale up benefits and reduce barriers to programme participation in the event of a disaster or other emergency. For example, in the United States, the Food Stamp Act requires the federal Government to establish such protocols for the country's largest food assistance scheme, the Supplemental Nutrition Assistance Program (SNAP). Following Hurricane Katrina, which hit the Gulf Coast in 2005, SNAP distributed at least US$585 million in benefits under temporary emergency rules that came into effect after initial assessments of the disaster. Programme eligibility and verification rules were relaxed and penalties were waived for administrative errors made during eligibility determinations (for subnational authorities, or states, participating in the federally-administered programme). Qualifying work requirements were waived and benefit payments were expedited and maximized for affected recipient households.

In Mexico's PET public works scheme, the Government can increase the maximum number and length of days participants are permitted to work, allowing them to earn additional income in the wake of a disaster.

CLIMATE FACTOR 3

Index-based triggers to activate or scale up payments complementing regular social protection transfers

Indices indicating seasonal or climate change-related hardships are used regularly in agricultural and livestock insurance schemes. Increasingly, they are also being looked at as triggers for top-up payments to social protection schemes that can be activated in the wake or anticipation of hardship. These types of mechanism are favoured for their speed in identifying hardship and triggering appropriate payments without the need to design and inaugurate new programmes to respond to each new incident. In some cases, systems are built such that payments are made with high levels of automation, leaving little need for intervention by programme administrators. Many of these indices are compiled from monitoring data on indicators, such as real and estimated rainfall, vegetation growth and livestock mortality, using a variety of sources, including observation satellites, weather stations and census data. For example, in Kenya, drought emergency scale-up payments complement a regular, unconditional cash transfer programme, the Hunger Safety Net Program (HSNP). In addition to regular payments, more than 90,000 households received drought-related payments in April and May of 2015.

The Government of Ethiopia operates the Productive Safety Nets Program, which offers a timely scale-up payment in anticipation of severe droughts or floods using a tool developed in collaboration with the World Food Programme. The Livelihoods, Early Assessment and Protection (LEAP) system assesses agro-meteorological data to estimate future crop yields and rangeland production.

Adequate financing arrangements to ensure resilience of social protection systems in times of crisis

Adequate financing arrangements must be developed to enable governments to implement social protection floors, including flexible aspects of anticipatory social protection programmes that ensure the resilience of the system in the face of rapidly increased demand related to a shock. While the core components of a social protection floor should be financed using domestic resources to ensure predictability and sustainability of the system, contingency financing may be arranged through international donor support or through nationally developed emergency reserves. For example, in Ethiopia, the Risk Financing Mechanism (RFM) provides funds in case of drought and the subsequent scale-up of the PSNP when needs exceed those that can be provided by the programme's regular contingency budget. This serves to ensure that the programme can absorb increased demand without undue budgetary pressures that might threaten future payments. In Kenya, the National Drought Management Authority (NDMA) operates the country's Disaster Contingency Fund (DCF), which finances county-led responses to droughts, including the distribution of emergency cash transfers. DCF funds are limited to financing emergency transfers and do not, to date, support drought emergency scale-up payments of the HSNP. It is expected that the inauguration of a National Drought and Disaster Contingency Fund (NDDCF) would replace the DCF, which may eventually serve as a unified contingency financing mechanism for both dedicated emergency response and emergency scale-ups under the HSNP.

5. Towards climate-ready social protection systems

In the Sahel, where social protection strategies are now emerging in several countries, there is a timely opportunity to support the articulation of nationally defined social protection floors that provide basic provisions, while integrating flexible components to provide protection against climate-related shocks and vulnerabilities.

Calls for social protection responses to remedy some of the negative effects of climate change and climate policies have made their way into several recent international agreements. For example, at the 21st session of the Conference of the Parties (COP 21) to the United Nations Framework Convention on Climate Change (UNFCCC) in December 2015 in Paris, one of the topics under discussion was "loss and damage", which for the first time yielded a dedicated article in the Paris Agreement (Article 8). The Agreement recognizes that climate change has tangible consequences on livelihoods. It does not, however, provide a basis for liability or compensation. Instead, it calls on countries to cooperate in areas like the development of early warning systems, disaster preparedness, risk assessment and management and different types of insurance, which could include social insurance and presumably other forms of social protection as part of social risk management, which make up a country's national social protection system.

The ILO, and many of its development partners within the United Nations system, are now tasked with integrating these and other considerations into the technical assistance the organizations provide in order to expand essential, sustainable social protection coverage and make systems more adept at protecting vulnerable populations with new and evolving circumstances related to the effects of climate change.

6. References

Bastagli, F.; Harman, L. 2015. The role of index-based triggers in social protection shock response (London, Overseas Development Institute).

The Cash Learning Partnership (CaLP). 2014. Is emergency cash transfer programming 'fit for the future'?.

European Commission. 2016. ECHO Factsheet – Sahel: Food & Nutrition Crisis.

Hobson, M.; Campbell, L. 2012. How Ethiopia's Productive Safety Net Programme (PSNP) is responding to the current humanitarian crisis in the Horn (Humanitarian Practice Network).

ILO. 2015. Outcome of the Tripartite Meeting of Experts on Sustainable Development, Decent Work and Green Jobs, Geneva, 5–9 Oct. (Geneva).

National Drought Management Authority, Kenya. 2016. Evaluation of the Kenya Hunger Safety Net Programme - Phase 2 (Nairobi).

Ovadiya, M.; Costella, C. 2013. Building resilience to disaster and climate change through social protection (Washington, DC, World Bank).

Richardson, J. 2006. Federal food assistance in Disasters: Hurricanes Katrina and Rita (U.S. Congressional Reporting Service).

World Bank. 2014. Helping poor families build resilience to climate change and other disasters in the Sahel. Available at: http://www.worldbank.org/en/news/feature/2014/07/15/helping-poor-families-build-resilience-to-climate-change-and-other-disasters-in-the-sahel.

12

South Africa: Social protection for children[27]

Of the 23 million children under the age of 18 in South Africa, about 60 per cent lives in poverty. The Child Support Grant, introduced in 1998, initially covered only 10 per cent of poor children. Incremental changes in the eligibility criteria and successful awareness-raising campaigns increased the coverage to 11.7 million poor children in 2015, or 85 per cent of the target group. The grant has been shown to have a positive impact on the recipient children and their families.

Social protection for children in South Africa is delivered through the Child Support Grant, Foster Care Grant, Care Dependency Grant, free education, school feeding and affordable health services. The CSG provides 330 South African Rands (ZAR) (27 US Dollars – US$) per month to poor children up to 18 years of age.

1. Main lessons learned

- South Africa has demonstrated that the extension of social protection to children is feasible and affordable for middle-income countries.
- Social grants for children complement services, such as free education, school feeding and affordable health services, thereby contributing to reduce poverty and vulnerability while ensuring that all children have access to nutrition, education and care.

---

[27] This chapter was authored by Thea Westphal of the ILO and reviewed by Isabel Ortiz, Valérie Schmitt, James Canonge and Loveleen De of the ILO. It was first published in February 2016.

- It is essential to have political will and commitment of the government particularly, to increase public expenditures on social protection. Today, South Africa redistributes roughly 3.5 per cent of its GDP through social assistance programmes.
- The creation of a specialized management institution, namely the South African Social Security Agency (SASSA), made delivery of social grants transparent and independent from political considerations.
- The Integrated Community Registration Outreach Programme (ICROP) helps people living in hard-to-reach and remote areas who are often excluded from receiving social protection benefits.

2. How is social protection provided to children in South Africa?

In 1913, the idea of providing income support to households with children was conceptualized by means of the Children's Protection Act, which provided for a State Maintenance Grant (SMG). The SMG was a means-tested grant paid to women who did not receive support from their partner or the child's father or who were in situations such as widowhood or desertion. Although all South Africans were legally eligible to receive the grant, people in the independent states where the black population lived were unable to access it because the states did not administer the benefit. The grant, therefore, effectively discriminated against the non-white population. Male family members often migrated to urban areas to find employment, leaving behind their families and breaking up traditional households. A main concern regarding the SMG and its focus on the nuclear family was that it did not fit the reality of many South African families.

After the end of the apartheid era, a reform of the social protection system was envisioned to meet the needs of multi- or skip-generation households where children were often raised by grandparents after parental migration or death from HIV/AIDS.

In 1998, the Child Support Grant (CSG) replaced the SMG and was designed to reach the child instead of being linked to the child's biological parents.

Figure 20: Coverage of the CSG in South Africa

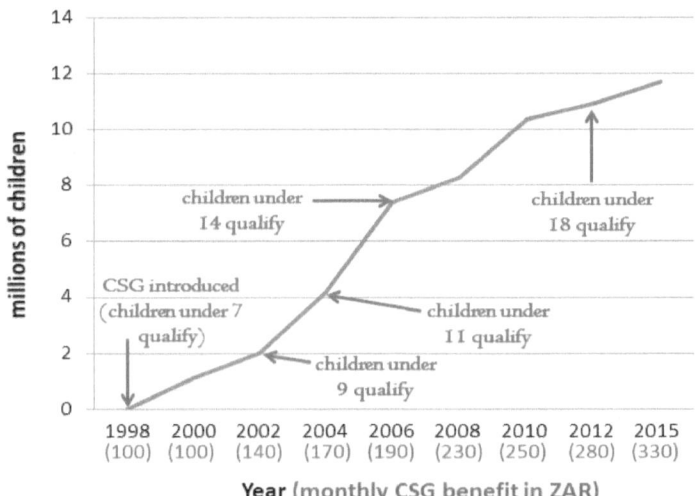

Source: Department for Social Development.

Initially, the CSG was a monthly benefit of ZAR100 (US$8) and covered children until 7 years of age. Over time, incremental changes were made to several features of the CSG programme.

The eligibility age was gradually increased to 18 years and the monthly benefit was raised to ZAR330 (US$27) per child. The monthly income threshold for the means test was raised to ZAR3,300 (US$269) for singles and ZAR6,600 (US$537) for couples. The CSG can be paid for up to six children, including legally or non-legally adopted children, as well as biological or non-biological children of the primary caretaker in a household.

Besides the CSG, South Africa provides a Foster Care Grant and a Care Dependency Grant. The Foster Care Grant is not means-tested, but has low coverage, which is often attributed to lengthy application procedures, including a court order confirming the child's need for foster care. The Care Dependency Grant provides ZAR1,410 (US$115) and the means test is ten times the benefit amount (monthly income threshold at ZAR14,100 or US$1,159). It is paid to children with severe chronic illnesses or disabilities, which have to be confirmed through a medical assessment. All grants are payable to citizens, permanent residents and refugees with legal status.

Figure 21: Recipients of child benefits in South Africa, 2015

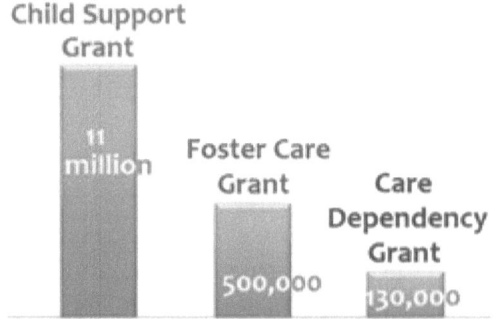

In addition to these grants, the Government provides complementary services in health and education.

3. What is the delivery mechanism?

In South Africa, two institutions are active in the design and delivery of social protection. The Department for Social Development (DSD) is responsible for policy-making and oversight while the South African Social Security Agency, created in 2006, administers and delivers all social grants. The creation of SASSA reduced fragmentation and inconsistency within the previous system, where the benefit levels and eligibility criteria for social grants were decided by nine different regions and disbursed by different paymasters.

Registration for the CSG requires children and their caretakers to submit their biometric data, including their photographs, fingerprints and voice recordings. This information, along with the beneficiary's name and a unique beneficiary identification number, are stored on an electronic chip card. This SASSA-branded MasterCard is the sole instrument used to identify beneficiaries.

Although it may take up to three months to process applications, benefits are paid retroactively from the date of application. Payments for all grants are made during the first two weeks of each calendar month. Payments are made through electronic bank transfers or by cash at SASSA offices, supermarkets or other payment points. When payments are made in cash, beneficiaries are identified through their SASSA-branded MasterCard.

Mobile payment unit   SASSA-branded MasterCard

Today, SASSA has registered all beneficiaries into a biometric electronic system and works with one paymaster. SASSA has gradually improved and made its payment system cost-effective by using biometric data and negotiating provider contracts. With the introduction of the smart card, the administrative cost decreased from ZAR33 (US$2.70) to ZAR16.4 (US$1.40) per month per beneficiary. Recording biometric data has allowed SASSA to identify 850,000 fraudulent grants.

A strong complaint and appeals mechanism underlies the social grant system in South Africa. Any decision of the implementing agency can be put to the Independent Tribunal for Social Assistance Appeals. It receives and hears appeals for all social grants, decides whether to confirm, alter or set aside a decision made by SASSA and whether to award the grant temporarily or permanently.

In addition to the use of technology and the establishment of complaint and appeals mechanisms, coverage was also increased through massive communication campaigns that sought to explain the benefits and eligibility criteria. These campaigns also tried to overcome traditional beliefs (e.g. infants have to stay at home during the first weeks after birth) that contributed to reducing registration rates for new-borns.

Further, the ICROP sought to increase coverage by helping people to complete applications forms and providing information. The ICROP uses fully functional mobile service units staffed with computers, office equipment and workers. These units travel to far-flung communities in the country.

4. What is the impact on people's lives?

In South Africa, since unemployment is high and poverty widespread, the CSG is spent primarily on food. The grant positively impacts health and nutrition of children. In fact, a study has found that children who benefit from the grant are, on average, 3.5 centimetres taller than non-recipient children.

The CSG also increases access to childhood development and schooling. Studies have shown that in CSG households, mothers are better informed of other services such as the early childhood development services, and are more inclined to register their children in these facilities. This has had positive consequences for the children since pre-school learning provides children a head start in education, improves their ability to develop social skills and allows the children to grow up in a safe environment.

Furthermore, the CSG has been shown to reduce incidences of risky behaviour among adolescents, such as reduced sexual activity, fewer pregnancies and reduced drug and alcohol use, especially for females.

Mothers in receipt of the CSG were more likely to participate in the labour market and more likely to be employed. Through the combined effects of improving school attendance and enabling mothers to participate in the labour market, the CSG has had a positive impact on the earnings of family members.

5. What's next?

South Africa has come a long way since the end of the apartheid era in 1994. Today, its social protection system is one of the most comprehensive in the region. While the CSG is currently a means-tested benefit, plans to raise the eligibility threshold and even universalize the grant are real policy options. Universal provision of the CSG will reduce many barriers to access and help include vulnerable children currently excluded from the programme.

6. References

DSD; SASSA; UNICEF. 2012. The South African Child Support Grant Impact Assessment. Evidence from a survey of children, adolescents and their households (Pretoria, UNICEF South Africa).

Education Training Unit. 2011. Social Welfare. Available at: www.paralegaladvice.org.za/docs/chap07/01.html.

Hagen-Zanker, J.; Morgan, J.; Meth C. 2011. South Africa's cash social security grants. Progress in increasing coverage (London, Overseas Development Institute).

Leubolt, B. 2014. Social policies and redistribution in South Africa, Global Labour University Working Paper No. 25 (Geneva, ILO).

SAHRC; UNICEF. 2014. Poverty traps and social exclusion among children in South Africa (Pretoria, SAHRC).

SASSA. n.d. Biometrics as a tool for fraud prevention and detection in the management of social assistance, PowerPoint presentation (Pretoria).

Senona, Engenas, Directorate Children and Family Benefits, Department of Social Development, Pretoria. 2015. Interview 6 May.

Statistics South Africa. 2014. Poverty trends in South Africa. An examination of absolute poverty between 2006 and 2011 (Pretoria).

Tiberti, L.; Maisonnave, H.; Chitiga, M.; Mabugu R.; Robichaud, V.; Ngandu, S. 2013. The economy-wide impacts of the South African Child Support Grant. A micro-simulation-computable general equilibrium analysis, Cahier de recherche/Working Paper 13-03 (Québec, Centre Interuniversitaire sur le Risque, les Politiques Economiques et l'Emploi).

13

Uruguay: Monotax[28]

An alliance between the social security institution and the tax collection authority promotes formalization and extends social security to independent workers

The creation of an administrative alliance between the tax authority and the social security institution, in order to establish a simplified and unified collection scheme for small contributors, allows for extended coverage to those enterprises that usually pay taxes, but are outside of the social security contributory system, or vice versa.

Monotax is a simplified tax collection/payment scheme for Uruguayan small contributors. People covered by the Monotax regime are entitled to the same social security benefits as salaried workers. The Monotax has proven to be an effective tool for the formalization of micro- and small enterprises, as well as for the extension of social security coverage to independent workers, especially women.

1. Main lessons learned

- The simplification of registration, collection of contributions, and service provision is increasing social security coverage.
- More flexible financing mechanisms can contribute to the formalization of the informal economy.

---

[28] This chapter was authored by Fabio Durán-Valverde of the ILO and reviewed by Isabel Ortiz, Valérie Schmitt and Karuna Pal of the ILO. It was first published in November 2014.

- Monotax has demonstrated the potential for a strategic alliance between social security institutions and tax authorities.
- One of the main characteristics of the Monotax is its impact in terms of gender. Women working in micro- and small firms, whether as employees or as employers, have the opportunity to be formalized and included in social security.
- The Monotax offers a solution to tackle the issue of low contributory capacity of informal economy workers.
- The Monotax is a successful model that is being implemented in other developing countries.

2. How was the Monotax set up?

The high level of coverage achieved by the social security system of Uruguay is largely the result of the nation's ability to introduce continuous innovations. The Monotax regime is an example of one of the innovations that has contributed to employment formalization and social security extension.

In the early 2000s, most Uruguayan independent workers were excluded from social security coverage, mainly due to inadequate legal framework and administrative procedures.

The Monotax was enacted in 2001, but 6 years after its introduction, its goals had not been achieved. In 2006 only 17.6 per cent of independent workers were covered by the social security system; therefore, the Monotax scheme undertook a profound reform. The changes, implemented in 2007, eliminated several restrictions on the conditions to join the scheme, including place of the activity, type of activity (such as "de facto" enterprises or not formally constituted businesses), maximum billing, among others.

Figure 22: Uruguay's Social Security Institute: Registration of Monotax enterprises and insured members

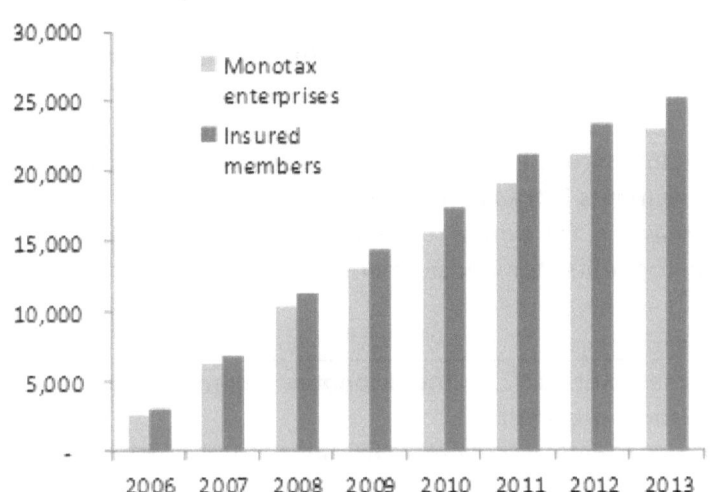

Source: Naranja, M. 2014. Monotributo. Descripción y análisis de su evolución. Montevideo, BPS.

It is worth mentioning that in 2011 the "Social Monotax" (*Monotributo Social MIDES*) was created as a special Monotax regime for one-person enterprises or joint entrepreneurship. Social Monotax can be accessed by individuals in households earning below the poverty line or in situations of socio-economic vulnerability.

3. What does the Monotax look like?

The Monotax was introduced in Uruguay in 2001 as an instrument to formalize the informal economy and to reduce exclusion from social protection of independent workers. It is a combined tax and social security contribution collection method for independent workers with limited turnover and with small commercial activities. It is focused on extending social security coverage to the informal economy.

Small businesses that fall into the category of Monotax contributors can choose between paying a "Monotax" (unified contribution) on revenue generated by their activities (called "Monotributo" in Spanish), or paying the ordinary social security contributions and normal taxes (with the exception of import taxes). Monotax contributions are collected by the Social Security Institute (BPS in Spanish) and the share corresponding to tax payments is transferred by the BPS to the fiscal authority. The remaining fraction is used by the BPS to finance social security benefits for those members affiliated through the scheme and their families.

Some characteristics of the Monotax regimes according to international practice:
- simplified taxation schemes aimed at combating informality;
- taxes and social security contributions are lower than general taxes in order to generate fiscal stimulus;
- taxable income is presumptive (presumed income in the absence of the information); a fixed fee is applied to each presumptive income category;
  taxes and social contributions are grouped in one contribution, the "Monotax";
- Voluntary registration and exit; beneficiaries may opt to join the general scheme;
- eligible beneficiaries are below a threshold or ceiling of income or gross sales;
- progressive and differential income categories.

Monotax members include one-person businesses, de facto non-family companies formed by a maximum of two partners with no employees, enterprises formed exclusively by family members (provided the number of partners is not over three), and companies with no salaried workers, under the condition of having a small income.

The micro-entrepreneurs who join the scheme are automatically entitled to the benefits of the contributory social security system (except for unemployment protection). There is some flexibility to encourage affiliation: while the contribution to pension coverage is mandatory, affiliation in the health insurance regime is voluntary and the entrepreneur can choose to make voluntary contributions to protect their children and spouse.

Contribution payments under the Monotax for pension insurance are gradually applied to new enterprises. They have three years to gradually meet the entire contribution rate.

MONOTAX scheme of URUGUAY

4. Formalizing the informal economy and impacting people's lives

Thanks to the innovative reforms associated with Monotax, in less than 3 years from the effective date of the new Law (June 2007), the number of enterprises and workers covered by the scheme has tripled.

The Monotax scheme has proven to be an effective instrument for the formalization and inclusion of independent workers into the social security system. Studies have shown that its implementation has reached low income groups of the population. More than 30 per cent of potential Monotax payers are covered by the Uruguayan social security system and over 20 thousand active enterprises are covered by the scheme. Although there is still a long way to go in terms of the extension of coverage, the implementation of the Monotax scheme has contributed to the goal of universalization.

Other similar experiences: Argentina, Brazil, and Ecuador

In Argentina, the Monotax has allowed for the subsidization of social security contributions for individual independent workers and micro-enterprises by incorporating low-income people into pension and health benefits schemes. In Brazil, SIMPLES (a simplified taxation scheme designed for micro- and small business) has significantly contributed to reducing the labour costs of micro-enterprises, promoting formalization of employment and growth. The *Régimen Impositivo Simplicado de Ecuador* includes a discount of 5 per cent in social security contributions for each affiliated worker, applicable to taxpayers who are up-to-date with payments.

Although this scheme is opened to both men and women, Monotax enterprises include a greater proportion of women— either as salaried workers or as employers. Women make up nearly 60 per cent of Monotax affiliates.

5. What's next?

The creation of the Monotax and its amendments have achieved the objective of extending social security. However, some challenges still remain. The coverage rate of independent workers in Uruguay is one of the highest in Latin America, but its levels are still far from 100 per cent.

The main challenge is to reach some categories of micro-enterprises that have not been reached by the existing Monotax schemes. In particular, the "Social Monotax MIDES" is an interesting option for reaching the poorest and most vulnerable groups in the informal economy.

6. References

Amarante, Verónica; Perazzo, Ivone. 2013. "Trabajo por cuenta propia y monotributo en el Uruguay", in Revista Internacional del Trabajo OIT, Vol. 132, No. 3-4, pp. 623-641. Available at: www.ilo.org/public/libdoc/ilo/P/09645/09645(2013-132-3-4)623-641.pdf.

Bertranou, Fabio (ed.). 2009. Trabajadores Independientes y protección social en América Latina (Santiago, ILO-BPS).

BPS. Evolución de los cotizantes, boletines 2010-2014 (Montevideo, BPS). Available at: www.bps.gub.uy/1940/evolucion_de_los_cotizantes.html.

Duran-Valverde, Fabio (Ed.) 2013. Innovations in extending social insurance coverage to independent workers. Experiences from Brazil, Cape Verde, Colombia, Costa Rica, Ecuador, Philippines, France and Uruguay (Geneva, ILO). Available at: www.socialsecurityextension.org/gimi/gess//RessourcePDF.acti on?ressource.ressourceId=42119.

Naranja Sotelo, Martín. 2014. Monotributo: Descripción y análisis de su evolución (Montevideo, BPS).

Santos, Silvia. 2014. Acciones con perspectiva de género en la seguridad social (Montevideo, BPS). Available at: www.bps.gub.uy/innovaportal/file/7883/1/43.20acciones20con 20perspectiva20de20genero20en20la20seguridad20social.20san tos.pdf

Annex 1: Social Protection Floors Recommendation, 2012 (No. 202)

PREAMBLE

The General Conference of the International Labour Organization,

Having been convened at Geneva by the Governing Body of the International Labour Office, and having met in its 101st Session on 30 May 2012, and

Reaffirming that the right to social security is a human right, and

Acknowledging that the right to social security is, along with promoting employment, an economic and social necessity for development and progress, and

Recognizing that social security is an important tool to prevent and reduce poverty, inequality, social exclusion and social insecurity, to promote equal opportunity and gender and racial equality, and to support the transition from informal to formal employment, and

Considering that social security is an investment in people that empowers them to adjust to changes in the economy and in the labour market, and that social security systems act as automatic social and economic stabilizers, help stimulate aggregate demand in times of crisis and beyond, and help support a transition to a more sustainable economy, and

Considering that the prioritization of policies aimed at sustainable long-term growth associated with social inclusion helps overcome extreme poverty and reduces social inequalities and differences within and among regions, and

Recognizing that the transition to formal employment and the establishment of sustainable social security systems are mutually supportive, and

Recalling that the Declaration of Philadelphia recognizes the solemn obligation of the International Labour Organization to contribute to "achiev[ing] ... the extension of social security measures to provide a basic income to all in need of such protection and comprehensive medical care", and

Considering the Universal Declaration of Human Rights, in particular Articles 22 and 25, and the International Covenant on Economic, Social and Cultural Rights, in particular Articles 9, 11 and 12, and

Considering also ILO social security standards, in particular the Social Security (Minimum Standards) Convention, 1952 (No. 102), the Income Security Recommendation, 1944 (No. 67), and the Medical Care Recommendation, 1944 (No. 69), and noting that these standards are of continuing relevance and continue to be important references for social security systems, and

Recalling that the ILO Declaration on Social Justice for a Fair Globalization recognizes that "the commitments and efforts of Members and the Organization to implement the ILO's constitutional mandate, including through international labour standards, and to place full and productive employment and decent work at the centre of economic and social policies, should be based on ... (ii) developing and enhancing measures of social protection ... which are sustainable and adapted to national circumstances, including ... the extension of social security to all", and

Considering the resolution and Conclusions concerning the recurrent discussion on social protection (social security) adopted by the International Labour Conference at its 100th Session (2011), which recognize the need for a Recommendation complementing existing ILO social security standards and providing guidance to Members in building social protection floors tailored to national circumstances and levels of development, as part of comprehensive social security systems, and

Having decided upon the adoption of certain proposals with regard to social protection floors, which are the subject of the fourth item on the agenda of the session, and

Having determined that these proposals shall take the form of a Recommendation; adopts this fourteenth day of June of the year two thousand and twelve the following Recommendation, which may be cited as the Social Protection Floors Recommendation, 2012.

I. OBJECTIVES, SCOPE AND PRINCIPLES

1. This Recommendation provides guidance to Members to:
    a. establish and maintain, as applicable, social protection floors as a fundamental element of their national social security systems; and
    b. implement social protection floors within strategies for the extension of social security that progressively ensure higher levels of social security to as many people as possible, guided by ILO social security standards.
2. For the purpose of this Recommendation, social protection floors are nationally defined sets of basic social security guarantees which secure protection aimed at preventing or alleviating poverty, vulnerability and social exclusion.
3. Recognizing the overall and primary responsibility of the State in giving effect to this Recommendation, Members should apply the following principles:
    a. universality of protection, based on social solidarity;
    b. entitlement to benefits prescribed by national law;
    c. adequacy and predictability of benefits;
    d. non-discrimination, gender equality and responsiveness to special needs;
    e. social inclusion, including of persons in the informal economy;
    f. respect for the rights and dignity of people covered by the social security guarantees;
    g. progressive realization, including by setting targets and time frames;
    h. solidarity in financing while seeking to achieve an optimal balance between the responsibilities and interests among those who finance and benefit from social security schemes;
    i. consideration of diversity of methods and approaches, including of financing mechanisms and delivery systems;

j. transparent, accountable and sound financial management and administration;

k. financial, fiscal and economic sustainability with due regard to social justice and equity;

l. coherence with social, economic and employment policies;

m. coherence across institutions responsible for delivery of social protection;

n. high-quality public services that enhance the delivery of social security systems;

o. efficiency and accessibility of complaint and appeal procedures;

p. regular monitoring of implementation, and periodic evaluation;

q. full respect for collective bargaining and freedom of association for all workers; and

r. tripartite participation with representative organizations of employers and workers, as well as consultation with other relevant and representative organizations of persons concerned.

II. NATIONAL SOCIAL PROTECTION FLOORS

4. Members should, in accordance with national circumstances, establish as quickly as possible and maintain their social protection floors comprising basic social security guarantees. The guarantees should ensure at a minimum that, over the life cycle, all in need have access to essential health care and to basic income security which together secure effective access to goods and services defined as necessary at the national level.

5. The social protection floors referred to in Paragraph 4 should comprise at least the following basic social security guarantees:

a. access to a nationally defined set of goods and services, constituting essential health care, including maternity care, that meets the criteria of availability, accessibility, acceptability and quality;

    b.   basic income security for children, at least at a nationally defined minimum level, providing access to nutrition, education, care and any other necessary goods and services;

    c.   basic income security, at least at a nationally defined minimum level, for persons in active age who are unable to earn sufficient income, in particular in cases of sickness, unemployment, maternity and disability; and

    d.   basic income security, at least at a nationally defined minimum level, for older persons.

6.   Subject to their existing international obligations, Members should provide the basic social security guarantees referred to in this Recommendation to at least all residents and children, as defined in national laws and regulations.

7.   Basic social security guarantees should be established by law. National laws and regulations should specify the range, qualifying conditions and levels of the benefits giving effect to these guarantees. Impartial, transparent, effective, simple, rapid, accessible and inexpensive complaint and appeal procedures should also be specified. Access to complaint and appeal procedures should be free of charge to the applicant. Systems should be in place that enhance compliance with national legal frameworks.

8.   When defining the basic social security guarantees, Members should give due consideration to the following:

    a.   persons in need of health care should not face hardship and an increased risk of poverty due to the financial consequences of accessing essential health care. Free prenatal and postnatal medical care for the most vulnerable should also be considered;

    b.   basic income security should allow life in dignity. Nationally defined minimum levels of income may correspond to the monetary value of a set of necessary goods and services, national poverty lines, income thresholds for social assistance or other comparable thresholds established by national law or practice, and may take into account regional differences;

     c. the levels of basic social security guarantees should be regularly reviewed through a transparent procedure that is established by national laws, regulations or practice, as appropriate; and

     d. in regard to the establishment and review of the levels of these guarantees, tripartite participation with representative organizations of employers and workers, as well as consultation with other relevant and representative organizations of persons concerned, should be ensured.

9.

     1. In providing the basic social security guarantees, Members should consider different approaches with a view to implementing the most effective and efficient combination of benefits and schemes in the national context.

     2. Benefits may include child and family benefits, sickness and health-care benefits, maternity benefits, disability benefits, old-age benefits, survivors' benefits, unemployment benefits and employment guarantees, and employment injury benefits as well as any other social benefits in cash or in kind.

     3. Schemes providing such benefits may include universal benefit schemes, social insurance schemes, social assistance schemes, negative income tax schemes, public employment schemes and employment support schemes.

10. In designing and implementing national social protection floors, Members should:

     a. combine preventive, promotional and active measures, benefits and social services;

     b. promote productive economic activity and formal employment through considering policies that include public procurement, government credit provisions, labour inspection, labour market policies and tax incentives, and that promote education, vocational training, productive skills and employability; and

    c. ensure coordination with other policies that enhance formal employment, income generation, education, literacy, vocational training, skills and employability, that reduce precariousness, and that promote secure work, entrepreneurship and sustainable enterprises within a decent work framework.

11.

    1. Members should consider using a variety of different methods to mobilize the necessary resources to ensure financial, fiscal and economic sustainability of national social protection floors, taking into account the contributory capacities of different population groups. Such methods may include, individually or in combination, effective enforcement of tax and contribution obligations, reprioritizing expenditure, or a broader and sufficiently progressive revenue base.

    2. In applying such methods, Members should consider the need to implement measures to prevent fraud, tax evasion and non-payment of contributions.

12. National social protection floors should be financed by national resources. Members whose economic and fiscal capacities are insufficient to implement the guarantees may seek international cooperation and support that complement their own efforts.

III. NATIONAL STRATEGIES FOR THE EXTENSION OF SOCIAL SECURITY

13.

    1. Members should formulate and implement national social security extension strategies, based on national consultations through effective social dialogue and social participation. National strategies should:

       a. prioritize the implementation of social protection floors as a starting point for countries that do not have a minimum level of social security guarantees, and as a fundamental element of their national social security systems; and

> > b. seek to provide higher levels of protection to as many people as possible, reflecting economic and fiscal capacities of Members, and as soon as possible.
> 2. For this purpose, Members should progressively build and maintain comprehensive and adequate social security systems coherent with national policy objectives and seek to coordinate social security policies with other public policies.

14. When formulating and implementing national social security extension strategies, Members should:
    a. set objectives reflecting national priorities;
    b. identify gaps in, and barriers to, protection;
    c. seek to close gaps in protection through appropriate and effectively coordinated schemes, whether contributory or non-contributory, or both, including through the extension of existing contributory schemes to all concerned persons with contributory capacity;
    d. complement social security with active labour market policies, including vocational training or other measures, as appropriate;
    e. specify financial requirements and resources as well as the time frame and sequencing for the progressive achievement of the objectives; and
    f. raise awareness about their social protection floors and their extension strategies, and undertake information programmes, including through social dialogue.

15. Social security extension strategies should apply to persons both in the formal and informal economy and support the growth of formal employment and the reduction of informality, and should be consistent with, and conducive to, the implementation of the social, economic and environmental development plans of Members.

16. Social security extension strategies should ensure support for disadvantaged groups and people with special needs.

17. When building comprehensive social security systems reflecting national objectives, priorities and economic and fiscal capacities, Members should aim to achieve the range

and levels of benefits set out in the Social Security (Minimum Standards) Convention, 1952 (No. 102), or in other ILO social security Conventions and Recommendations setting out more advanced standards.

18. Members should consider ratifying, as early as national circumstances allow, the Social Security (Minimum Standards) Convention, 1952 (No. 102). Furthermore, Members should consider ratifying, or giving effect to, as applicable, other ILO social security Conventions and Recommendations setting out more advanced standards.

IV. MONITORING

19. Members should monitor progress in implementing social protection floors and achieving other objectives of national social security extension strategies through appropriate nationally defined mechanisms, including tripartite participation with representative organizations of employers and workers, as well as consultation with other relevant and representative organizations of persons concerned.

20. Members should regularly convene national consultations to assess progress and discuss policies for the further horizontal and vertical extension of social security.

21. For the purpose of Paragraph 19, Members should regularly collect, compile, analyse and publish an appropriate range of social security data, statistics and indicators, disaggregated, in particular, by gender.

22. In developing or revising the concepts, definitions and methodology used in the production of social security data, statistics and indicators, Members should take into consideration relevant guidance provided by the International Labour Organization, in particular, as appropriate, the resolution concerning the development of social security statistics adopted by the Ninth International Conference of Labour Statisticians.

23. Members should establish a legal framework to secure and protect private individual information contained in their social security data systems.

136. Innovations to extend coverage

24.

    1. Members are encouraged to exchange information, experiences and expertise on social security strategies, policies and practices among themselves and with the International Labour Office.

    2. In implementing this Recommendation, Members may seek technical assistance from the International Labour Organization and other relevant international organizations in accordance with their respective mandates.

Annex 2: Sustainable Development Goals related to social protection

Goal 1
End poverty in all its forms everywhere
Target 1.3
Implement nationally appropriate social protection systems and measures for all, including floors, and by 2030 achieve substantial coverage of the poor and the vulnerable

Goal 3
Ensure healthy lives and promote well-being for all at all ages
Target 3.8
Achieve universal health coverage, including financial risk protection, access to quality essential health-care services and access to safe, effective, quality and affordable essential medicines and vaccines for all

Goal 5
Achieve gender equality and empower all women and girls
Target 5.4
Recognize and value unpaid care and domestic work through the provision of public services, infrastructure and social protection policies and the promotion of shared responsibility within the household and the family as nationally appropriate

Goal 8
Promote sustained, inclusive and sustainable economic growth, full and productive employment and decent work for all
Target 8.5
By 2030, achieve full and productive employment and decent work for all women and men, including for young people and persons with disabilities, and equal pay for work of equal value

138. Innovations to extend coverage

Goal 10
Reduce inequality within and among countries
Target 10.4
Adopt policies, especially fiscal, wage and social protection policies, and progressively achieve greater equality

Annex 3: ILO standards on social protection

The up-to-date ILO Conventions and Recommendations on social security or social protection are listed below:

- The Social Security (Minimum Standards) Convention, 1952 (No. 102), which covers all nine branches of social security and sets minimum standards for these nine branches;
- The Income Security Recommendation, 1944 (No. 67) and the Medical Care Recommendation, 1944 (No. 69) , which envisage comprehensive social security systems and the extension of coverage to all and laid the foundations for Convention No. 102 (1952).

Other up-to-date Conventions and Recommendations, adopted after Convention No. 102 (1952), set out higher standards for particular branches of social security. Drawn up on the model of Convention No. 102, they offer a higher level of protection, both in terms of the population covered and of the level of benefits, as follows:

- The Medical Care and Sickness Benefits Convention, 1969 (No. 130) and the Medical Care and Sickness Benefits Recommendation, 1969 (No. 134) makes provision for medical care and sickness benefit;
- The Employment Promotion and Protection against Unemployment Convention, 1988 (No. 168) and the Employment Promotion and Protection against Unemployment Recommendation, 1988 (No. 176) relates to unemployment benefit;
- The Invalidity, Old-Age and Survivors' Benefits Convention, 1967 (No. 128) and the Invalidity, Old-Age and Survivors' Benefits Recommendation, 1967 (No. 131) covers old-age benefit, invalidity benefit and survivor's benefit;

- The Employment Injury Benefits Convention, 1964 (No. 121) and the Employment Injury Benefits Recommendation, 1964 (No. 121) makes provision for employment injury benefit;
- The Maternity Protection Convention, 2000, (No. 183) and the Maternity Protection Recommendation, 2000 (No. 191) covers maternity benefit;
- The Equality of Treatment (Social Security) Convention, 1962 (No. 118), the Maintenance of Social Security Rights Convention, 1982 (No. 157) and the Maintenance of Social Security Rights Recommendation, 1983 (No. 167) provide reinforced protection to migrant workers; and
- The Social Protection Floors Recommendation (No. 202) provides guidance for the establishment and maintenance of social protection floors and their implementation within strategies for the extension of social security aiming at achieving comprehensive social security system.

These instruments can be consulted in the Database of International Labour Standards. (NORMLEX)

www.ingramcontent.com/pod-product-compliance
Lightning Source LLC
Chambersburg PA
CBHW021943170526
45157CB00003B/903